The Black Archive ...

THE ULTIMATE FOE

By James Cooray Smith

Published November 2017 by Obverse Books

Cover Design © Cody Schell

Text © James Cooray Smith, 2017

Range Editor: Philip Purser-Hallard

2

For Swyrie and Danuka.

The other Cooray Smiths.

Also Available

CONTENTS

OVERVIEW

Serial Title: *The Trial of a Time Lord* Parts 13 to 14, aka 'The Ultimate Foe'

Writer: Robert Holmes (episode 1 / Part 13), Pip and Jane Baker (episode 2 / Part 14)

Director: Chris Clough

Original UK Transmission Dates: 29 November – 6 December 1986

Running Time: Episode 1 / Part 13: 24m 42s

Episode 2 / Part 14: 29m 30s

UK Viewing Figures: Episode 1 / Part 13: 4.4 million

Episode 2 / Part 14: 5.6 million

Regular Cast: Colin Baker (The Doctor), Bonnie Langford (Melanie)

Recurring Cast: Michael Jayston (The Valeyard), Lynda Bellingham (The Inquisitor), Tony Selby (Glitz), Anthony Ainley (The Master)

Guest Cast: Geoffrey Hughes (Popplewick), James Bree (Keeper of the Matrix)

Antagonists: The Valeyard, the Master

Novelisation: *Doctor Who: The Trial of a Time Lord – The Ultimate Foe* by Pip and Jane Baker. **The Target Doctor Who Library #131**.

Sequels and Prequels: *Dragonfire* (TV, 1987), *Head Games* (novel, 1995), *Millennial Rites* (novel, 1995), *The Eight Doctors* (novel, 1997), *Mission: Impractical* (novel, 1998), *Matrix* (novel, 1998), *He Jests at Scars...* (audio, 2003), *Trial of the Valeyard* (audio, 2013), **The Sixth Doctor: The Last Adventure** (audio, 2015)

Responses:

'The Ultimate Foe is fantastic **Doctor Who** in every way. It demonstrates everything the show does **so** well.'

[Joe Ford, *The Doctor Who Ratings Guide*]

'Never before (and I hope never again), have I come away from a **Doctor Who** story wishing it had never been made, but it was that bad. I suppose the only way to rectify it would be for the Doctor to wake up and find it was all a bad dream. Bad it was; dream it unfortunately wasn't.'

[Paul Scoones, 'The Trial of a Time Lord', *Time and Space Visualiser* #1]

SYNOPSIS

(**The Doctor** is on trial for his life, charged with interfering in the affairs of other cultures, his case to be judged by an **Inquisitor** and a panel of senior Time Lords. The prosecutor, **the Valeyard**, is seeking a death sentence. He has presented as evidence visual records from the Matrix, the Time Lords' repository of knowledge, of two of the Doctor and **Peri**'s recent experiences. In the first, they encountered **Glitz**, a criminal attempting to steal a cache of data on a devastated future Earth[1]. The second apparently saw the Doctor behaving with uncharacteristic ruthlessness which led to Peri's death[2]. In his defence, the Doctor has presented a record relating to a future adventure with a new associate, **Mel**, in which he will apparently destroy an entire species. He disputes the truth of these accounts, insisting that the Matrix data has been falsified. The Valeyard has insisted that the defendant should now be charged with genocide[3].)

Episode 1 / Part 13

The Inquisitor summons **the Keeper of the Matrix**, who assures those present that nobody without the Key he holds could possibly enter the Matrix. This is almost immediately belied by the appearance on the Matrix data feed of **the Master**, who has gained access using a duplicate Key. He has also summoned Mel and Glitz to act as the Doctor's defence witnesses.

Glitz testifies that the data he was attempting to steal on the

---

[1] *The Trial of a Time Lord* Parts 1 to 4, aka 'The Mysterious Planet'.
[2] *The Trial of a Time Lord* Parts 5 to 8, aka 'Mindwarp'.
[3] *The Trial of a Time Lord* Parts 9 to 12, aka 'Terror of the Vervoids'.

Master's behalf was originally appropriated from the Matrix, and that the Time Lords' own High Council devastated the Earth to eradicate the rogue information. More shockingly, the Master reveals that the Valeyard is the Doctor himself – an amalgamation of the darker sides of his nature at a future time. The Master confirms that the Valeyard has doctored the evidence at the High Council's behest, in return for control over the remainder of the Doctor's incarnations. By revealing the conspiracy, the Master hopes to bring down the High Council, and to set the two versions of his nemesis against one another.

The Valeyard flees through a door into the Matrix itself, and the Doctor and Glitz follow him, into an unreliable dreamscape fraught with murderous illusions. In a building called the Fantasy Factory they meet a Dickensian clerk, **Mr Popplewick**, who tries to obstruct them from meeting his superior, an identical Mr Popplewick. After the Doctor signs his remaining lives away to the Factory's proprietor, 'JJ Chambers', Popplewick instructs him to await their appointment with Chambers. The waiting room is a bleak beach where disembodied subterranean hands pull the Doctor down into quicksand.

Episode 2 / Part 14

The Doctor easily frees himself from the illusion, and is rewarded with a confusing conversation with an illusory Valeyard, who explains that he needs to kill the Doctor to free himself from the constriction of the latter's moral scruples. He then releases non-illusory toxic nerve gas at the Doctor and Glitz, who take shelter in a cottage which turns out to be the Master's TARDIS.

The Master is concerned that the Valeyard, no longer handicapped by the Doctor's ethics, will be an unbeatable opponent. He incapacitates the Doctor and uses him as bait to draw the Valeyard out of the Fantasy Factory, but the Valeyard does not fall for the trick. The Doctor is lured by an illusory Mel to a facsimile of the Time Lord courtroom. The ersatz Inquisitor finds him guilty and condemns him to death, while Mel watches horrified from the real courtroom. She steals the Keeper's Key, enters the Matrix and rescues the Doctor – to his annoyance, as he was well aware the courtroom scene had been faked, and had been hoping to meet the Valeyard.

Meanwhile on Gallifrey, the High Council has been deposed. Still speaking from the Matrix, the Master attempts to fill the power vacuum. Glitz breaks into the Fantasy Factory and discovers the originals of the Matrix data whose pirated versions he previously tried to steal. The Master forces him to surrender them, and attempts to access them through his TARDIS console – only to set off a booby-trap which incapacitates him and Glitz.

The Doctor and Mel are taken by Popplewick to Chambers's office, where they tie him up and unmask him as the Valeyard. The Doctor discovers that the Valeyard has built a particle disseminator capable of killing all the Time Lords in the courtroom, via the Matrix visual feed. He disables it and escapes, and the machine explodes, apparently killing the Valeyard.

The Inquisitor tells the Doctor that, according to the Master, Peri is still alive, and he and Mel leave in the TARDIS. As the courtroom clears, the Keeper of the Matrix is revealed as a disguised Valeyard.

NOTES ON TERMINOLOGY

The **title** of this book, in keeping with **Black Archive** house style, refers to the two instalments of **Doctor Who** transmitted as '*The Trial of a Time Lord* Part Thirteen' and '*The Trial of a Time Lord* Part Fourteen' as 'The Ultimate Foe'. For a discussion of the rights and wrongs of this, please see Appendix 1: Title Fight.

Black Archive house style would normally refer to these instalments of **Doctor Who** as 'The Ultimate Foe' episodes 1 and 2. As this book will be discussing the first 12 instalments of *The Trial of a Time Lord* (1986) as well as the final two, it will use the 'Part' terminology and the full numbering. Thus, the story under discussion here consists of 'Part 13' and 'Part 14', and any references made to 'Part 1' and 'Part 2' will be to the first two instalments of *The Trial of a Time Lord* (alternatively known as 'The Mysterious Planet' episodes 1 and 2).

PRODUCTION TIMELINE

4 February 1986

Parts 13 to 14 commissioned from Robert Holmes as 'Time Inc'.

24 February 1986

Jonathan Powell demands extensive changes to Parts 1 to 4. Work on Part 13 suspended as a consequence.

6 March 1986

Parts 9 to 12 commissioned from Pip and Jane Baker as 'The Ultimate Foe'.

13 April 1986

Eric Saward formally resigns as **Doctor Who**'s Script editor.

24 May 1986

Robert Holmes dies.

4 June 1986

Eric Saward withdraws his replacement version of 'Part 14'.

6 June 1986

Pip and Jane Baker are commissioned to write a new 'Part 14'.

23 to 24 June 1986

Location Recording at Camber Sands (Matrix/Beach).

30 June to 3 July 1986

Location Recording Pottery Museum (Fantasy Factory).

16 July 1986

Studio Recording Television Centre Studio 1 (TARDIS set).

17 July 1986

Studio Recording Television Centre Studio 1 (Court sets).

19 August 1986

14 episodes of **Doctor Who** ordered for 1987.

29 October 1986

Colin Baker's contract is not renewed for 1987's episodes.

28 November 1986

John Nathan-Turner informed he will produce 1987 series if he wishes to remain a BBC staff producer.

29 November 1986

Colin Baker appears on BBC's **Saturday Superstore** to promote Part 13.

29 November 1986

Part 13 transmitted.

6 December 1986

Part 14 transmitted.

13 December 1986

Colin Baker's departure from **Doctor Who** announced.

CHAPTER 1: ON TRIAL

On Thursday 28 February 1985 the populist UK tabloid *The Sun* ran as its front page headline 'Dr Who Axed In Plot by the BBC'. The story, which had been leaked through intermediaries by *Doctor Who*'s then Producer, John Nathan-Turner, was a response to his having been informed that week by his head of department, Jonathan Powell, that the 1986 series of **Doctor Who** would not be going ahead as planned.

Mere days before, Nathan-Turner had dismissed internal BBC rumours to this effect when they were put to him by his Script Editor Eric Saward, and his meeting with Powell came as an enormous shock, both professionally and personally.

> 'John came down almost in tears. His baby had been snatched. He was **really** upset [...] He zoomed in, and I thought "I wonder what's happened there?" He did something in his own office, then came over to me, said "This is what's happened... I've got to go and lie down now." And went back into his office; and about an hour later we had a chat about it. That was the first he knew, and then I knew a few minutes later. It mortified him, he was really, really upset, he didn't know what to do.'
>
> [Eric Saward][4]

---

[4] Saward, Eric, interviewed by Ed Stradling, Richard Molesworth and Richard Legree for use on the BBC **Doctor Who** DVD range, 14 December 2006. Much of the material remains unpublished, and I have worked from a transcript. All quotes from Saward are, unless otherwise footnoted, taken from this interview.

Within hours, the Producer had decided he did know what to do: he would come out fighting. He leaked the series' cancellation to *The Sun*'s Charles Catchpole ahead of an official public announcement. Ian Levine, a long-time **Doctor Who** fan who was at the time close to the production office, actually made the call to the tabloid newspaper, using a known Fleet Street codeword for BBC insiders leaking internal matters to the press, while Nathan-Turner sat opposite him, writing down the information he wanted Levine to pass on[5]. Calls to other papers followed. Publication deadlines meant that the first paper covering the story to hit the stands was *The Standard*, which ran it as a front page item on the evening of Wednesday 27[6].

Nathan-Turner's gambit worked. Knowing from calls from the press that Thursday's newspapers would be full of the story, and what the tone of that coverage would be, BBC Drama rushed an announcement out themselves: a statement ahead of the leak which had itself been made ahead of their planned statement. The BBC **Six O'Clock News** and **Nine O'Clock News** bulletins on Wednesday 27 March carried news of **Doctor Who**'s not cancellation but 'postponement', with both programmes insisting that the then-current series of **Doctor Who** would not, in fact, be the programme's last.

Earlier that day Powell, BBC One Controller Michael Grade, and

---

[5] Levine, Ian, speaking on 'Trials and Tribulations' (extra on 'The Ultimate Foe' DVD release).

[6] Patrick Hill, 'Dr Who Fails to Make the Grade', *The Standard*, 27 March 1986. *The Standard* is now *The London Evening Standard*, and as the name implies, it is now, as then, an evening paper aimed at London's commuters. It has had no morning edition since 1916.

Head of BBC Press Keith Samuels had had a meeting with Bill Cotton, the Corporation's Managing Director. (Powell describes himself as 'summoned' to the discussion.) The embarrassment of the imminent press coverage was discussed, as was a further financial matter that had been raised internally. **Doctor Who** was, in theory, part-funded by BBC Enterprises, the corporation's commercial wing. In practice, Enterprises' contribution to **Doctor Who**'s budget was more than was actually spent on the programme, with some of the money being used on other productions entirely. Cancelling **Doctor Who** would mean that the Enterprises money would no longer be transferred over to the Drama department, meaning programmes other than **Doctor Who** would face a shortfall of funds following **Doctor Who**'s cancellation. Powell also recalls an apparent threat by a **Doctor Who** fan group to picket BBC Television Centre, which prompted Samuels to say:

> '"This is what you're going to have to do, you're going to have to make some more shows, because if they do that it'll be on the front page of every newspaper in the world," and we kind of went, "Oh God, make another series".'[7]

Nathan-Turner's initial dismissal of rumours which turned out to be wholly accurate is, in its proper context, completely understandable. Pre-production of the 1986 series of **Doctor Who** was well underway, with at least six 45-minute scripts complete or nearing completion, directors and guest artists booked and location dates for the opening serial 'The Nightmare Fair', scripted by

---

[7] Marson, Richard, *JN-T: The Life and Scandalous Times of John Nathan-Turner*, p241.

Nathan-Turner's predecessor as Producer, Graham Williams, already arranged. Aborting these serials in such an advanced stage of pre-production would involve considerable cost without a single second of television to show for the money paid out. Doing so would make no financial sense.

It would also be against all known BBC Drama procedure. Nathan-Turner would have inevitably been aware that BBC Drama's commissioning and budgeting was done on a rigid annual schedule, and that the time for decisions about programmes intended for transmission in January 1986 was now well past. He also found it inconceivable that the cancellation of any series would be undertaken by higher management without any consultation with that series' own production office.

And yet he was wrong. Because while under normal conditions, a decision about a programme for the coming January would not – and as Nathan-Turner understood **could** not – be made in the February of the financial year prior, during the winter of 1984-85 'normal conditions' had been quietly suspended. Late 1984 had seen Grade, an executive hugely experienced in commercial television but who had never worked at the BBC, appointed to run the channel. By his own account Powell had a strong desire to indicate to Grade, who commenced work at the BBC in December, his personal willingness to accommodate his new superior's tastes and interests in his department's output, even if it meant the substantial redrawing of already made and costed plans. Thus the axe fell on **Doctor Who**, wholly outside the normal processes of programming commissioning and budgeting, at a cost to the BBC

Drama department of very slightly under £90,000[8].

This happened, very simply, because both Powell and Grade thought **Doctor Who** was not the kind of programme the BBC should be making in the mid-1980s[9]. Earlier in his career, while an executive at London Weekend Television, Grade had routinely used **Come Dancing** (1950-98) and **Doctor Who** as totemic examples of tired BBC programmes that demonstrated how the corporation had failed to move with the times[10]. And as for Powell:

> 'I don't know what [Powell] thought of **Doctor Who** before he arrived [at the BBC] but he **hated** it, no two ways about it. We would walk in, and his face dropped. He used to sit on the sofa for the producer's playback and he nodded off on one occasion. If he'd said something you would have at least been able to go somewhere [with his feedback], but it was just this disdain... He **loathed** it.'
>
> [Eric Saward]

---

[8] Marson, *JN-T*, p234. This is approximately a quarter of a million pounds in early-21st-century values.

[9] Alternative explanations, related to, for example, the cost to BBC drama of launching **EastEnders** (1985-) are comprehensively dismissed by David Reid in Marson, *JN-T*, p224, and do not require repeating here.

[10] Ironically, both series are key parts of the BBC One Saturday night line up in the second decade of the 21st century.

'Jonathan, when he became the Head of Department, felt he only wanted to make the kind of television that he liked, and my own view is that is not the role of the Head of Department.'

[David Reid][11]

A flamboyant figure with a public profile, it was Grade, not Powell, that bore the brunt of public and media scorn for their joint decision to cancel **Doctor Who**. Most stories about the cancellation singled Grade out for attention. Several punned on his name in headlines or subheadings. Many sought to portray Grade as, in effect, the latest and greatest in **Doctor Who**'s long catalogue of villains, equating his attempt to end the programme with their fictional attempts to kill its eponymous lead.

Grade and Powell's decision, taken in haste and against procedure,

---

[11] 'Trials and Tribulations'. Reid was Powell's immediate predecessor as Head of Drama Series and Serials. A television writer since 1969, he had also come from the commercial sector, having been a senior figure in drama at ATV. He was not only a producer on **Sapphire and Steel** (1979-82) but was also responsible for ATV buying the series in the first place, having been hugely impressed by PJ Hammond's 25-minute pilot script. These facts may be seen to help explain his greater sympathy with the challenges of making a family fantasy series like **Doctor Who** in a low-budget videotape environment. In 1983 he had insisted to Nathan-Turner that incoming star Colin Baker committed to at least four series of **Doctor Who**, as he felt Peter Davison's tenure in the role had been too brief. Saward has described Reid thus: 'a nicer, more charming person I've yet to meet, he was friendly, supportive, encouraging, all the things you would hope for [in a superior].'

was swiftly reversed because of, perhaps even in, their meeting with Cotton and Samuels, and Powell would, in later years, express disbelief at his and his colleagues' cowardice in not standing by their decision.

Much of the press coverage of **Doctor Who**'s 'cancellation crisis' mentioned that Grade was unavailable for comment, as he was on holiday, with *The Times* of 1 March specifying that he was skiing in France. Given that Grade had been present in the meeting that Wednesday morning, it is hard to interpret his sudden desire to be on the piste as anything other than running away from the over-personalised press controversy **Doctor Who** had unexpectedly generated.

Other BBC employees, too, were keen to avoid the subject if at all possible. On the morning of 28 February Frank Bough, presenting the **Breakfast Time** television magazine programme, stopped discussion of the BBC's **Doctor Who** embarrassment during the regular 'What the Papers Said' slot, initially joking that he 'hardly dare speak about **Doctor Who** [...] my job is in jeopardy'. Then, when his guest, the actress Gwen Taylor, pressed on with discussing the series regardless, Bough pointedly referred to his earpiece adding, 'Someone has just said in my ear "I think that's enough on **Doctor Who**,"' before abruptly changing the subject[12]. The topic of **Doctor Who** was clearly a sore point within the Corporation at the end of that week, and how it was discussed was of concern to those with 'front-facing' roles within the organisation.

---

[12] Bough, Frank, speaking on '1985 Hiatus' (extra on 'The Ultimate Foe' DVD release).

This, though, did not prevent a brief skit on the matter being staged on that Friday's edition of **Wogan**. The sketch featured the programme's presenter Terry Wogan[13] and David Banks as a Cybercontroller[14]. The joke that Grade was simply the latest **Doctor Who** villain was expanded, with the Cybercontroller praising Grade as an ally who should be 'Cybernised' as a reward for achieving something the Cybermen never had: The defeat of the Doctor[15].

That same day, Friday 1 March 1985, only the day after the *Sun* story appeared, Bill Cotton formally communicated via the BBC press office that there **would** be a 1986 series of **Doctor Who**. It would start later in the year than originally intended, with transmission pushed back from January to the autumn. Cotton's announcement also revealed that the programme would once again be made as 25-minute episodes, the 1985 series having been produced, experimentally, in the 45-minute format even then more common for drama for adults. Crucially, it stated that reverting to the 25m format would allow the series to be aired for 'a greater

---

[13] Sir Terry Wogan (1938-2016) was a notable friend to **Doctor Who** throughout his career in British broadcasting, involving the programme in the annual **Children in Need** telethon which he hosted, and interviewing key figures from the series on his chat show. He was also a fan of **Doctor Who**'s spiritual sibling **Blake's 7** (1978-81).

[14] Banks played the Cyber**leader** in four **Doctor Who** stories from *Earthshock* (1982) to *Silver Nemesis* (1988), but for his **Wogan** appearance he wore the Cybercontroller helmet made for Michael Kilgariff in *Attack of the Cybermen* (1985).

[15] It is in some ways extraordinary, and unequivocally to the corporation's credit, that Grade could be publicly mocked on the flagship chat show of the channel over which he was the ultimate authority.

number of weeks'[16].

Officially speaking, this postponement or 'suspension' was very quickly all that had ever been intended, and this period swiftly became known in fan argot as 'the 18-month hiatus' (although in practice, it only involved the 1986 series' start date being pushed back by nine months). Nathan-Turner would for the rest of his life maintain that 'a hiatus' was the worst-case scenario for **Doctor Who** in 1985.[17] He may have come to believe that to be the case. Powell has since indicated more than once that, despite what was said after the leak to the papers, it absolutely was both his and Grade's intention that the then-current series of **Doctor Who** would be the programme's last[18], with the series concluding with the Eric-Saward-scripted *Revelation of the Daleks*, due to be transmitted in the last two weeks of March 1985. (Both Colin Baker and Eric Saward have separately since acknowledged that the situation was initially explained to them as outright cancellation of the programme[19].)

> 'We **did** try to cancel it, there was Bill Cotton, the Managing Director, Michael [Grade] and myself, the Head of Drama[20].

---

[16] Lee, Harvey, 'BBC Buys £¾m Mini-Series after Dr Who Decision', *The Daily Telegraph* 2 March 1985.

[17] E.g. in Nathan-Turner, John, 'Listen, Do You Want to Know a Secret?' Doctor Who Magazine (DWM), #240.

[18] Marson, *JN-T*, pp230-245.

[19] Squaring this is not difficult. The original 1986 series **was** cancelled. Its costs were written off and its productions aborted. A new 1986 series, one made in a different financial year, was then commissioned **after** the furore, and this would not have happened without it.

[20] Powell was, in fact, only Head of Drama Series and Serials at this

But I remember the reaction was so severe.'

[Jonathan Powell][21]

Any ambiguity in Grade's feeling about **Doctor Who** was probably dissipated when, on 2 March 1985 and after four uninterrupted days of often highly personalised press criticism[22], his holiday was interrupted when *The Daily Mail* successfully tracked him down to the French Alps, and pressed him for comment against his will while he was in public with his family. It is in these comments that Grade first claimed that **Doctor Who**'s 'suspension' was related to falling viewing figures, a claim that doesn't really stand up when comparing 1985's numbers to the years immediately prior[23]. (Grade would return to this point in the 23 to 29 March issue of *Radio Times*, in a response to a letter criticising his decision[24].)

The Daily Mail's intervention in Grade's personal life marks the first time he was prepared to go publicly and overtly on the offensive at the slight on his professional judgement that criticism of his cancellation of **Doctor Who** represented, and the near

---

point, but he would be promoted again shortly.

[21] 'Trials and Tribulations'.

[22] Had he seen it, he might have been justifiably outraged by *The Scotsman* newspaper's 1 March 1985 allegation that the cancellation/postponement of **Doctor Who** was related to the corporation's then-recent purchase of the right to screen Embassy Films' **Kane & Abel** (1985), on which Grade had been a producer while still working in the commercial sector, and the unfounded, arguably libellous, implication that this situation was in some way corrupt.

[23] Honan, Corinna, 'Grade: Why the Doctor Had to Go'. *Daily Mail*, 2 March 1985.

[24] Letters, *Radio Times*, cover date 23-29 March 1985.

demonisation of him in the press during that week[25]. It would not be the last. Among many examples he called the 1985 series 'tired and unimaginative'[26] and was quoted as saying, 'The people who make it have got rather complacent, they got rather violent and lost a lot of its imagination, a lot of its wit and was relying far too much on straightforward on-the-nose violence.'[27]

It is a moot point whether the sheer scale of Grade's publicly-expressed disdain for the series was the result of the publicity surrounding his 1985 actions or the opinion that prompted them. The public criticisms above, and the many others like them he made over a period of months, may merely represent boredom at being repeatedly asked about **Doctor Who** (a single programme, which formed a tiny part of Grade's remit, which was not even on the air for almost all of Grade's tenure at BBC One); equally they may reflect a resentment of its survival as a challenge to his authority and/or be a genuine personal diagnosis of the programme as it existed in 1985. Most probably, they constitute a mixture of all three.

It is little wonder that, against such a background, Nathan-Turner and Saward were left feeling that 'the hiatus' was a condemnation of their work on the series. Because, and despite assurance made to them internally that this was not the case, it clearly was. Their superiors had attempted to end their programme, at significant cost and outside normal BBC procedures, because they disliked it,

---

[25] For example, *The Daily Mail* of 1 March devoted both its cartoons and an article to pillorying Grade professionally and personally in relation to **Doctor Who.**

[26] *The Times*, 14 January 1986.

[27] *The Stage and Television Today*, 17 October 1985.

and felt its budget could be better spent elsewhere. Accordingly, both men thought it likely they would not be in charge of **Doctor Who** when it returned in the autumn of 1986.

> 'I thought John might be demoted or put on another show. And I thought they would cancel my contract[28] and that would be it. My removal wasn't asked for.'
>
> [Eric Saward]

In the end, both Nathan-Turner and Saward remained in post. Bad publicity had forced BBC Drama to continue **Doctor Who**, but there would have been no tabloid outcry had its Producer and Script Editor, people whose names were largely unknown to the general public, been moved onto other BBC series and their roles on **Doctor Who** taken by other BBC staff or contractors. Yet this did not happen, with neither Nathan-Turner nor Saward moved to make way for an appointee more to Powell's liking.

> 'There wasn't anybody else around... There was no natural line of succession that I could remember seeing. I had no ideas. Also, what was I going to do with fucking John Nathan-Turner?'[29]

---

[28] The BBC at the time was still organised more like a civil service department than any other organisation. Nathan-Turner was a permanent member of staff, but Saward was a contract worker (albeit one doing a staff job) whose contract needed to be formally renewed by his department every few months or it would lapse.

[29] In both this interview and Marson's (*JN-T*, p245) Powell occasionally demonstrates what might reasonably be thought to be a specific animosity against Nathan-Turner as an individual, as well as an employee. (Powell was, it is fair to say, openly unconvinced of Nathan-Turner's merit as a producer.) It is possible, although

[Jonathan Powell][30]

Moreover, Nathan-Turner was a staff producer. Terrance Dicks, **Doctor Who**'s Script Editor from 1968 to 1975, and by 1985 a BBC Drama staff producer himself, has indicated that it was essentially 'impossible' to remove a staff producer from his job[31] 'unless he urinated on the Director General's desk or something'[32].

> 'I couldn't find anyone else to do it. I didn't know what I was going to do with **him** if he wasn't going to do it.'
>
> [Jonathan Powell][33]

---

neither man ever indicated as such, that this hostility originated in the period when both were staff producers in the same department, and nominal equals. Saward certainly regards Powell's dislike as personal, saying 'I know he didn't like us. It wasn't just him not liking the show, he didn't seem to like **us**.'

[30] Marson, *JN-T*, p256. In fact, BAFTA-winning children's television producer Clive Doig, who had worked on the series in junior capacities in the 1960s, was interested in taking over the programme, mentioning this to his departmental superiors on more than one occasion.

[31] 'His job' as distinct from 'his current role'. Staff Producers were often moved from one series to another by department heads under the system then in place.

[32] Cook, Benjamin, '"He Never Gives In And He Never Gives Up... He is Never Cruel or Cowardly"', DWM #508, February 2017. Nathan-Turner, in fact, remained at the BBC until the staff producer role ceased to exist in 1990, and he was made redundant, spending his final year without a programme to make, and instead effectively working as the BBC's **Doctor Who** licensing and merchandise approval manager, from his old production office.

[33] 'Trials and Tribulations'. Powell is perhaps misremembering here. Former BBC producer Terence Dudley, then working as a freelance

27

Powell was probably unaware that Nathan-Turner was considering his own position, and the latter would later ponder whether he should have resigned from the BBC entirely at this point[34]. With the BBC publicly committed to another series, had he removed himself from the Producer's chair BBC Drama would have had to have appointed a successor. Saward, for his own part, came to feel in retrospect that he too had made a mistake in staying:

> 'I thought "If I go now, it will look as though I'm running away," so I stayed and I think that was a mistake – I should have gone. I should have left on my own personal small high of *Revelation* [*of the Daleks*][35], it would have been a good time to go.'

Something which is rarely acknowledged in discussion of this period of **Doctor Who**'s history is that, if Grade and Powell thought **Doctor Who** was a bad television programme, and as such a waste of BBC

---

writer and director, wrote to BBC Drama on 16 July 1985 expressing an interest in producing the series, while Terrance Dicks (see above) has frequently since intimated that he would have taken the job had it become available during his time as a BBC producer (1985-89), and that he would have enjoyed working with incumbent star Colin Baker. It might be conjectured that Powell saw Dudley, who had both written and directed for the series under Nathan-Turner, and Dicks, a writer and producer with a long association with the series in several media, as too close to the programme.

[34] E.g., when interviewed by Bill Baggs for the 1994 documentary *The Doctors*. Much of the material remains unpublished and I have access to a transcript, courtesy of Ed Stradling.

[35] Saward's favourite amongst his **Doctor Who** scripts and arguably the most fully worked through example of the series as he wanted it to be.

resources, then they had not only the right, but arguably a **duty**, to cancel it. The production and scheduling of BBC Drama Department productions was, jointly, their responsibility. It was quite literally their jobs. Comments by both about the content of **Doctor Who**, made in the aftermath of the events of February 1985, almost certainly reflect both their genuine professional opinions of the series, and their reasons for attempting to end it[36].

What is also worth acknowledging is that, whatever their professional judgments, they also had a duty to observe professional **standards** when implementing those judgements. Had they wanted to axe **Doctor Who** in early 1985, the proper way to go about that would have been to refuse the production office's 'offer' to the department for a January 1987 series, during the spring 1985 'offers round'. Yes, that would have meant one more series of a programme neither liked, but it was a series that had already been budgeted and, largely paid for, and much of the money could not be recouped[37]. They would at least have had 13

---

[36] Colin Baker, who has more reason than any to feel bitterness towards Grade and Powell, has noted Grade 'did what in his opinion was right for the BBC. I didn't like what he did, obviously, but [...] He just did his job as he saw it.' ('An Interview with Colin Baker, *The Whostorian Blog*, 22 August 2012.)

[37] Colin Baker has since revealed that BBC Drama did attempt to 'wriggle out' of paying him his fee for the cancelled series, as per his contract. They were possibly unaware that as well as being an actor Baker is a qualified solicitor. (Baker, Colin, interviewed by Ed Stradling, Richard Molesworth and Richard Legree for use on the BBC **Doctor Who** DVD range, 14 December 2006. Much of the material remains unpublished, and I have worked from a transcript. All quotes from Baker are, unless otherwise footnoted, taken from this interview.)

more hours of television for that money, and probably avoided a public scandal on the scale of the one their unorthodox cancellation technique provoked.

They would also have had to wait all of six weeks to take the decision in this way.

When a very public scandal dictated that Doctor Who **had** to continue to be made despite both men's wishes, they again had not simply the right, but also a duty, to make it as good as they thought it could be. Again, they were high-ranking BBC staff members, who were (well) paid to make logistical and creative decisions about BBC programming. Given Powell's contempt for Nathan-Turner, and Saward's feeling that this dislike also extended to him, that logically should have involved the removal of the series' Producer and Script Editor. This did not happen. In fact, Grade and Powell allowed the series to continue under a Producer in whom neither had any faith, and whom Grade was prepared to publicly criticise. It's another, equally strange but curiously diametrically opposite, failure of professional standards. It was probably equally rooted in the pair's joint dislike for both the series and its producer, and almost certainly in part prompted by resentment at media responses to, and portrayals of, them exercising the functions of their jobs[38].

Managerial refusal to engage with what they perceived to be creative problems with **Doctor Who** at this stage, instead allowing

---

[38] For all the flagrant unorthodoxy of Grade and Powell's attempt to end **Doctor Who**, there was surely no other BBC production, drama or otherwise, that could have prompted such a reaction to its cancellation. **Dixon of Dock Green** (1955-76) had gone quietly into the great goodnight after 22 series a decade earlier without a public scandal.

a programme which they had been publicly embarrassed into allowing to be made to continue without making efforts to improve it, is itself arguably a dereliction of their professional duty, as both public-sector workers and creative figures. Had overt, dramatic managerial intervention become a kind of hostile neglect? Maybe. Perhaps there was more to it than that. Maybe Powell, if not Grade, felt that **Doctor Who** and John Nathan-Turner deserved one another.

> 'I wanted **him** to fuck off and solve it – or die, really. If he'd solved it fine, but it had probably gone beyond solving.'[39]

> [Jonathan Powell]

So it was that, in the absence of being pushed, both Nathan-Turner and Saward declined to jump, erring on the side of caution and, quite understandably, of assured continued employment. Both men might also have, quite justifiably, felt that they now had something to prove to their superiors, if not the world at large.

And then, for a quarter of a year, nothing happened. The unseemly public brouhaha about **Doctor Who** was followed by three months in which both Nathan-Turner and Saward felt largely unable to do any new work on the 1986 series, unsure of what was now required of them.

> 'Much to my amazement we were still sitting there three months later. I can't remember what I was doing for the

---

[39] Marson, *JN-T*, p235. As a remark it is all the more surprising in its frankness for having been made not only after the success of 21st-century **Doctor Who** illustrated that the series was not 'beyond solving', but also after Nathan-Turner's premature death at the age of 54.

three months[40], after having been so busy to suddenly have nothing, but yes, I did turn up. They were paying me.'

[Eric Saward]

In May Nathan-Turner and Saward finally had a single, brief meeting with Powell and Grade, in which the management's creative concerns about **Doctor Who** were finally discussed[41]. The Producer and Script Editor were told that the 1985 series had been too violent, and that the 1986 series should be more humorous. 'A lot of these accusations came later, when they were looking for reasons,' comments Saward. On another occasion, he would note that in his opinion three 1985 stories, *Vengeance on Varos*, *The Two Doctors* and *Revelation of the Daleks* were 'very comic'[42]. Little else in terms of advice or feedback was offered from either the Head of Department or the Controller of BBC One. The programme would be permitted to continue but, counterintuitively, in almost exactly the form that had seemingly prompted Powell and Grade to take such extraordinary measures to end it.

---

[40] The limited amount of production paperwork related to these months supports Saward's depiction of an office effectively paralysed by recent events.
[41] Saward has estimated that the meeting lasted around 10 minutes in total.
[42] Saward, Eric, 'The Revelations of a Script Editor'. *Starburst* #97, p16.

'Finally we were told we had to come up with a relaunch for the show, that was all. Nothing about what they wanted... no indication as to how they wanted this relaunch to be handled.'

[Eric Saward]

'I'm not conspiracy-theorist, I'm cock-up theorist. I suspect [Grade] thought it would just disappear without too much fuss... suddenly he had to justify it, so along came the "Too much violence. Not enough humour," after waiting **weeks**... two sentences, which they [Nathan-Turner and Saward] did their best with.'

[Colin Baker]

Some progress was made on **Doctor Who**'s new creative direction when Nathan-Turner pitched to Grade and Powell Saward's idea of a linking theme for the new series: a run of stories in which the Doctor would be placed on trial by his own people for his actions as an adventurer in time and space. The story idea had come from Saward's partner Jane Judge's observation that the series and its production team were in effect 'on trial'[43]. Saward himself has since described the concept as prompted 'more by desperation than creativity' and 'not my best idea', but the approach was nevertheless accepted by Powell and Grade. (Star Colin Baker felt 'some pause about the wisdom' of the fictional trial echoing the programme's real-life woes, but this was assuaged by his colleagues.)

---

[43] Judge was also professionally familiar with the **Doctor Who** production office, having previously been production secretary to both Nathan-Turner and his predecessor Graham Williams.

Another aspect of Saward's concept, one possibly more to the well-read Baker's liking, was his decision to loosely base the structure of the 1986 series, and the Doctor's trial, on that of Charles Dickens's 1843 novella *A Christmas Carol*. The first story would show the Doctor in the (recent) past, the second his actions immediately before being brought to trial, and the last section a possible future for the character, should he be acquitted. With the Doctor's trial echoing the programme's, there seems to have been a desire for a story that would demonstrate, on more than one level and to more than one audience, **Doctor Who**'s inherent worth and right to continue to exist – to continue indeed to have new adventures, in both a fictional and a metafictional sense.

May 1985 also brought confirmation that the 1986 series would consist of 14 episodes of 25m duration. As the 1985 series had consisted of 13 episodes of 45m, this fulfilled Cotton's public statement that the series would run 'a greater number of weeks', but was also a near-halving of **Doctor Who**'s screen time.

The 'Trial' idea finally killed off the 'on the shelf' scripts commissioned and in some cases completed for the cancelled 1986 series, as they would have required substantial rewriting to become part of Saward's 'Trial' concept. Initially, Nathan-Turner had hoped to include some of the scripts they had already bought in the revised season, telling *Doctor Who Magazine* (DWM) 'We have more than enough scripts to choose from. Some we may use, in fact we may use them all – we haven't decided.'[44] (This,

---

[44] Marson, Richard, 'Interview: John Nathan-Turner and Eric Saward', DWM #108. On 7 March 1985 Nathan-Turner briefed BBC Copyright to extend the options on several already-commissioned scripts, leading to new fees for the writers, demonstrating this was

apparently, was a bigger issue than them representing a vision of the series their departmental superiors considered a failure, perhaps due to the ambiguity with which that opinion had been expressed internally[45].) The writing of the 1986 series would have to begin again.

Scripts for a 4 X 25m first serial (given the BBC production code 7A, previously allocated to 'The Nightmare Fair') were formally commissioned from Robert Holmes[46], and a second (7B) from Philip

---

more than an idle thought. In the same interview he portrayed the period in which Saward subsequently described the production office as paralysed as a 'quite nice, just for a change [...] if we don't feel like talking on a Wednesday we can talk on a Thursday. Normally it has to be a Wednesday because Thursday and Friday we'd be in the studio.' The producer also indicated that he would shortly take the leave he had built up due to **Doctor Who**'s excessive schedule.

[45] Graham Williams' 'The Nightmare Fair' would, had it been made for the revised 1986 series, have had to be 'bought again', even if no further changes had been made to the scripts by the author. The then-standard BBC 'production window' between a script's' commission and any transmission date would have been exceeded.

[46] Robert Holmes (1926-86) was himself a former **Doctor Who** Script Editor, and his contributions to the series are the standouts of a long career writing series television, chiefly crime and science fiction. Holmes still wrote for **Doctor Who**, nearly 10 years after leaving its permanent staff: his contribution to the 1985 series, *The Two Doctors*, was in mid-transmission when Nathan-Turner was informed of the series' cancellation, the second of its three episodes having gone out on 22 February. Indeed Saward says it was from Holmes that he heard the initial rumours about **Doctor Who**'s cancellation which Nathan-Turner had so blithely dismissed. (Holmes had heard them from a secretary who worked on the BBC's higher-managerial 'sixth floor'.)

Martin[47] on 2 September 1985, after both men had already begun work on their stories[48]. Both were writers who had written for **Doctor Who** within the last year, whose work Saward admired, and with whom he enjoyed working, and he accepted their submissions in due course. However, getting completed scripts for the final six episodes of the series would prove a far from easy process. Scripts and storylines for potential two-part stories were commissioned from David Halliwell[49] and Jack Trevor Story[50], and when these fell through, four-part stories were commissioned from, successively, PJ Hammond[51] and Christopher H Bidmead[52] before being written

---

[47] Martin (born 1938) is a Liverpudlian playwright and screenwriter, best known for the surreal BBC crime drama **Gangsters** (1975-78).

[48] All eight scripts had a projected delivery date of 14 October 1985.

[49] David Halliwell (1936-2006) is best known for the play *Little Malcolm and His Struggle Against The Eunuchs* (1967) and its film adaptation (1974), both of which starred his RADA contemporary, and future Doctor, John Hurt in the title role.

[50] Jack Trevor Story (1917-91) was an incredibly prolific prose fiction writer, and *Guardian* newspaper columnist, whose *The Trouble With Harry* was adapted to film by Alfred Hitchcock in 1957.

[51] Peter J Hammond (born 1930) is a television writer with a specific personal style invoking folk myth and memory, one best expressed in his own series, the aforementioned **Sapphire and Steel** (1979-82), but which he has been able to apply to programmes as disparate as **Z-Cars** (1962-78), **Ace of Wands** (1970-72) and **Midsomer Murders** (1997-). He would later write two episodes for the 21st-century **Doctor Who** spin-off **Torchwood** (2006-11), *Small Worlds* (2006) and *From Out of the Rain* (2008).

[52] Christopher H Bidmead (born 1941) is an actor, journalist and screenwriter, and was Saward's immediate predecessor as **Doctor Who**'s (full-time) Script Editor. Author of three of the most admired 1980s **Doctor Who** serials, *Logopolis* (1981), *Castrovalva* (1982) and

off. Finally, Pip and Jane Baker[53], who had written *The Mark of the Rani* for the 1985 series, were commissioned to write a four-part story briefed as 'An Agatha Christie in space', in early February 1986.

It may seem surprising that some of the 'written-off' but originally approved serials for the aborted 1986 series were not resurrected at this point, given the clear desperation for usable scripts. While the 'Trial' format may have been restrictive, adapting them would not have proved as difficult as getting new scripts seems to have become. The answer lies in production resources: The first four episodes, made as a single production ('7C') with the final two episodes of the series, were required to be shot entirely in studio. 'The Nightmare Fair' and 'The Hollows of Time' scripts in particular would have required extensive location work. Philip Martin's 'Mission to Magnus' would have been an all-studio production, but producing it as '7C', even as an emergency contingency, would have meant two successive Martin-scripted adventures, in both of which Sil was the antagonist.

Saward had always intended that the final two episodes of 7C, and of the 1986 series as a whole, would also be written by Holmes, whose scripts for Parts 1 to 4 had deliberately left dangling plot

---

Frontios (1984), his contribution to the originally-projected 1986 series, 'The Hollows of Time', was formally written off in summer 1985, after scripts were completed.

[53] Philip Baker and Jane Baker (d. 2014) were a husband-and-wife screenwriting team, often working in children's television (such as **Watt on Earth** (1991-92)) and science fiction (e.g. **Space: 1999** *A Matter of Balance* (1976)).

threads for the writer himself to return to at the series' climax[54]. Two 25m scripts, for the 13th and 14th episodes of the series, were commissioned from Holmes on 4 February 1986, two months before his now-completed scripts for 7A were due to be recorded.

It was at this point that things began to go **really** wrong.

---

[54] While this was not the first time that 20th-century **Doctor Who** attempted a 'series finale' in the now widely used sense (*The War Games* (1969), *The Dæmons* (1971) and *The Armageddon Factor* (1979) are earlier examples) it was the first time the it had done so when facing the possibility of cancellation. There was every chance that Holmes' episodes would be the programme's, as well as the series', final instalments, and this was public knowledge (e.g. Hewson, David, 'BBC Keeps Option Of Killing Doctor Who', *The Times*, 14 January 1986). The cross-plotting of the 'Trial' is also arguably more involved than even that of the 1978-79 'Key to Time' series, making this sort of storytelling, at this time, new ground for **Doctor Who**.

CHAPTER 2: PART 13 BY ROBERT HOLMES

The script of the transmitted version of Part 13 is credited solely to Robert Holmes, but he is by no means the only person to have written scenes contained within the finished episode. There are several overlapping reasons for this, all of which are worth some discussion. Holmes' work on the newly-commissioned Parts 13 and 14 was almost immediately interrupted when on 24 February 1986 Jonathan Powell, in his capacity as Head of Department, issued a comprehensive set of notes on the scripts for Parts 1 to 4, scripts which Holmes regarded as finished with, following Saward's own formal acceptance of them on 15 January[55].

Holmes was the most prolific, one of the longest-serving, and probably the most admired of 20th-century **Doctor Who** writers, and Saward has labelled Powell's dismissal of Holmes' scripts as 'disrespectful'[56]. (A feeling which was perhaps exacerbated by Powell's minimal notes on Philip Martin's scripts, which he praised and approved with minor changes.) Powell, though, had been a **hugely** creatively successful producer within BBC Drama before

---

[55] Some of these notes are reprinted in Molesworth, Richard, 'Bob's Fantasy Factory'. *Nothing at the End of the Lane* #4.

[56] Holmes is, indeed, the only one of **Doctor Who**'s Script Editors to write extensively for the series before, during and after his time in the position. Most others either built up to the job and then left it behind, or came in new and then stayed around as an experienced hand. Gerry Davis (with one serial, heavily rewritten, seven years after leaving) and Dennis Spooner (six episodes within months of leaving and a second, brief script-editing stint the year after) are minor counterexamples.

being promoted into his managerial role[57], and giving notes as and when he chose was part of his current job, whether Saward liked it or not.

Significantly, some of his implemented suggestions for these episodes are unequivocally improvements. Powell thought Glitz and Dibber, who were on Ravolox to steal Queen Katryca's jewels, had insufficient motivation for their 'caper' and were not well integrated into the rest of the story. This led to the creation of the 'Black Light Converter' that powers Drathro's complex, and Glitz's attempts to destroy it in order to salvage it for scrap, linking the story's plot threads more closely. Powell is unlikely to have known that two conmen stealing royal jewels was a story Holmes had already used in **Doctor Who** (*The Ribos Operation* (1978)) although this in itself would have been a sound reason to revise the scripts. He also asked for the removal of the Doctor's many 'yard' puns on the Valeyard's title, an aspect of the serial that has been routinely criticised since its transmission.

Holmes and Saward began reworking the earlier episodes in line with Powell's comments, delaying work on Parts 13 and 14. By the time he could turn his attentions to Part 13 once more, Holmes had become ill (by Saward's account he had contracted a form of

---

[57] A producer on Granada's daytime drama **Crown Court** (1972-84) in the early 1970s, Powell moved to the BBC and produced a string of outstanding drama serials, including the Dennis-Potter-scripted **The Mayor of Casterbridge** (1978), **Tinker Tailor Soldier Spy** (1979), **Testament of Youth** (1979) and **The Barchester Chronicles** (1982). These inarguable achievements led to his promotions to Head of Drama Series and Serials, Head of Drama and Controller of BBC One within five years.

hepatitis from contaminated shellfish)[58], suffering a swift and visible decline in his health noted by friends and colleagues such as Robert Banks Stewart and Chris Boucher[59]. Saward communicated to the Bakers, who were by this point writing Parts 9 to 12, that 'Holmes was having terrible difficulties with episode 14 and he felt he just couldn't write it.'[60] Shortly after he submitted his first draft of Part 13, Holmes was admitted to Stoke Mandeville Hospital. It quickly became clear to Saward that Holmes '...wouldn't be fit enough to write Episode 14'[61]. 'It was apparent that he was not going to get better, so I couldn't just leave things hoping he would return to work in a couple of days' time'. Having fallen into a coma Holmes died a few weeks later, on 24 May 1986, while Saward was writing his own version of the conclusion they had planned together.

In late 1985 Saward had been told, in line with standard BBC policy, that as the series' Script Editor he wouldn't be able to write any of the 1986 series of **Doctor Who** himself[62]. However, the exceptional circumstance of a terminally-ill screenwriter constituted sufficient cause for an exception to the rules to be granted. By Saward's

---

[58] Saward, Eric, Part 13 DVD commentary.

[59] Molesworth, Richard, *Robert Holmes: A Life in Words*, pp419-20.

[60] Marson, Richard, 'Pip and Jane Baker: Strange Matters'. DWM #137.

[61] Saward, Part 13 DVD commentary.

[62] Saward's previous scripts for the series had been commissioned before he was made Script Editor (*The Visitation* (1982)), nominally edited by someone else (*Earthshock*), or commissioned by Nathan-Turner during periods when Saward, a contract worker and thus ostensibly not BBC full-time staff, was 'out of contract' pending its renewal (*Resurrection of the Daleks* (1984), *Revelation of the Daleks*).

account Nathan-Turner was nevertheless reluctant to let his Script Editor write the final episode himself, and had to be pushed into realising there really was no alternative. Saward agreed, on the proviso he be allowed to follow the 'vague outline' that he had agreed with the then-hospitalised Holmes[63]. The Producer seemed amenable.

Before beginning work on Part 14, however, Saward decided to substantially redraft Holmes' submitted draft for Part 13. It cannot have been an easy decision for Saward, given his respect for Holmes and the state of the elder writer's health, to do as he did and discard almost 50% of Holmes's material in the process of his rewrite. It is difficult to be certain why Saward felt this to be necessary. Perhaps plausible reasons can be found by looking at the material itself.

We can do this, because Holmes' initial draft of Part 13 exists. It survives as a single, typed, foolscap document of 21 pages, of which I have been allowed to access a digital copy. It makes for interesting reading. The title page has 'DOCTOR WHO' in the top left corner and 'Episode 13' underneath it, with about six carriage returns separating the two. The absolute centre of the page reads 'THE FANTASY FACTORY'.

The script is divided into 13 scenes, eight 'scenes' and five 'Telecines' (a contemporary term for any scene not shot on videotape (VT) at a BBC studio[64]), which are numbered separately.

---

[63] Saward, Part 13 DVD commentary.
[64] The term itself relates to the use of the film, rather than video, medium to capture the material. For 1986 **Doctor Who** moved to using video, rather than film, for exterior as well as interior

The first four scenes of Holmes's script, and a special effects Telecine, are present, with some amendments, in the final episode. Holmes's Scene 7 is also present, almost wholly unaltered, in the final episode. (In the final rehearsal script for the episode, it has become Scene 6 due to the rearrangement of other material.) The rest of the episode was written by other hands – principally, although not entirely, Saward's.

Comparisons enumerated below are with the transmitted version of the episode, which is available on DVD. (Referring to 'Appendix 2: Scene Breakdowns' may help clarify some detail in the remainder of this chapter.)

Holmes's draft opens with an effects Telecine, one which shows a single 'casket' specified as resembling 'the ornate objects sold on the US death market', travelling down the light beam that brought the TARDIS to the Trial Station at the start of Part 1[65]. We then cut to the Courtroom, where both Melanie and the Keeper of the Matrix are already present[66]. (The transmitted episode begins with

---

sequences, having experimented with doing so as early as 1974. (Film was still used for some model and special effects work, including the shot of the space station seen in Part 13.) Nevertheless all scripts for the 1986 series, regardless of their author, designate location work as 'Telecine', the terminology not having caught up with the technology.

[65] This shot is moved slightly later in the televised version, in which there are, in order to accommodate other changes to the script, two caskets, not one.

[66] David Halliwell's notes from July 1985 indicate that the Keeper was originally intended to be present in the court throughout the 1986 series (Molesworth, 'Bob's Fantasy Factory'), and Holmes' draft seems to work on this assumption. The Keeper, there given

Melanie not present in the Courtroom and the Keeper arriving under the closing moments of the opening credits music[67]). Holmes' draft of this scene contains dialogue for Melanie[68], who is seated to the Doctor's left and whose arrival in the courtroom he clearly anticipated having been dealt at some point in Parts 5 to 12. This early dialogue was removed along with the character, rather than reallocated to other characters.

Onscreen dialogue referring to Part 12's cliffhanger, and the Valeyard's accusation of genocide, are not yet present in the script[69], but aside from these interpolations the televised scene is entirely Holmes' work. There are also some cuts which are of interest. The Inquisitor states that the Valeyard has now 'concluded his case' and asks 'Do you have any defence to offer at all, Doctor?' Clearly Holmes had not been informed that Parts 9 to 12 would, as written by the Bakers, consist of the Doctor making a presentation to in his own defence, and expected them to also consist of prosecution evidence[70]. The transmitted Scene 1 ends with the

---

the name Zon, does appear as a (largely silent) character in Philip Martin's novelisation of his own scripts for Parts 5 to 8 (Martin, Philip, *Mindwarp* p6 and passim).

[67] The transmitted Part 13 runs 24m 42s, near the upper limit for a BBC programme in a 25m slot.

[68] E.g. 'It's obviously a put up!' and 'A frame up from beginning to end!' with reference to the Doctor's trial.

[69] Parts 9 to 12 were then being written, and Holmes could not have been aware of their content. These lines were probably added by either Nathan-Turner or the Bakers themselves, as Saward had left the production office before Part 12 was delivered.

[70] This is also in keeping with Martin's *Mindwarp* novelisation, based on slightly longer, slightly earlier drafts than those used for recording. Martin's book concludes with the Valeyard informing the

Doctor's line 'Such as [...] the Valeyard!', when the moved and amended Telecine 1 is cut to, but here the Inquisitor has additional dialogue informing the Doctor that such an accusation could lead to him facing an additional charge of contempt, before we cut to Scene 2[71].

Holmes' Scene 2 shows Sabalom Glitz clambering out of the casket that has arrived outside the Courtroom, and consists of a single line of dialogue ('What I do for grotzis...'). This was amended by Saward to have a second casket present containing Melanie, and dialogue where the two introduce themselves was added, along with an acknowledgement that Dibber, Glitz's sidekick from Parts 1 to 4, is absent and that this absence is, from Glitz's point of view, unanticipated[72].

---

court that the 'final section of the prosecution – the future' is imminent, saying:

> 'Doctor, we have seen you active in the far past. As to your recent activities – we have just witnessed your ineptitude. We had no choice but to extract you from the consequences of your dangerous meddling.'

When the Doctor says he has seen the error of his ways, and will change The Valeyard replies:

> 'No, Doctor you do **not** change [...] Sagacity, I will demonstrate that in a possible future the Doctor continued to be the same interfering destroyer of the delicate fabric of time.'

> [Martin, *Mindwarp*, p140.]

[71] This material was recorded, and is included as part of the 'Deleted Scenes' package on the *Trial of a Time Lord* DVD set.

[72] Curiously, Holmes, who created Dibber, does not mention him. It may be that he intended to deal with the character's fate in his Part 14.

Scene 3 returns to the Courtroom. Although almost all of the material in this scene as written is present onscreen, and there is essentially nothing onscreen that does not come from this draft, Scene 3 is perhaps the most textually interesting section of Holmes' script. The first point of interest is that dialogue present in this version, but excised before or during recording, is present in the novelisation of these two episodes, which was written by Pip and Jane Baker in 1988. There are half a dozen lines of dialogue in this scene alone where the novelisation corresponds with Holmes' draft rather than the transmitted version of the episode or the final rehearsal script[73]. This is far too many for coincidence.

There is a second, even more telling, similarity between Holmes' draft and the Bakers' novelisation which neither share with the transmitted programme: in the first draft and the prose retelling, the revelation of the Valeyard's identity **precedes** the Doctor's cross-examining of Glitz about the history of Ravolox. In the finished episode, and in John Nathan-Turner's own copy of the rehearsal script, filed at the BBC Written Archive at Caversham, the details of the High Council's attack on Earth are discussed **first**, and the revelation of the Valeyard's identity causes the Doctor's trial to collapse, with the prosecutor escaping across the courtroom and into the Matrix as the Inquisitor attempts to restore order[74].

---

[73] E.g. the Bakers reassign Melanie's observation – rather cruel, under the circumstances – that the Valeyard is 'Very like [the Doctor] round the eyes' and her 'When I saw him I thought to myself –' to Glitz (who finishes the latter thought with 'this Valeyard must be the Doc's brother!'), but the thought (or joke) is retained (Baker, Pip and Jane, *The Ultimate Foe* p27).

[74] BBC Written Archives Centre (WAC) file T/65/164, rehearsal

Given this, it seems certain that pages 10 to 54 of the Bakers' novelisation represent an intermediate draft of the script, after Saward's rewrites of the Matrix material, but before the one represented by the finished programme and the camera script filed at the BBC's Written Archive[75]; one where Scene 3 retains the sequence of events from Holmes' original script.

The positional reversing of the two central, long sections of Scene 3 is undoubtedly to the drama's benefit, and was a sensible editorial decision. But who made it? Saward has indicated that Holmes's original plan, and Nathan-Turner's request, was that 'The Master was going to be the villain of the piece,' and that it was Saward himself who felt that:

> 'The Valeyard is the natural villain – once you've established that he is the Doctor in a later incarnation you have to go with that, and what he's prepared to do to get what he wants.'

This may be the reason for the switch, and if so it is a logical one. The revelation that the Valeyard is the Doctor is a huge moment, in terms of both character and story, and returning immediately afterwards to the cut and thrust of pseudo-legal argument in order to rake over the minutiae of plot points from 10 episodes before

---

script (undated).

[75] The novelisation also contains a moment when the Inquisitor summons the Keeper of the Matrix and he arrives shortly afterwards, which seems like a natural mid-way point between Holmes' draft having him always having been in the Courtroom and the transmitted episode's treatment of his arrival (Baker and Baker, *The Ultimate Foe* pp12-13).

feels dramatically wrong both in Holmes's draft and in the Bakers' novelisation[76].

However, the page numbering of Nathan-Turner's copy of the rehearsal script for Part 13 indicates that the decision to swap these sections of Scene 3 was made after it was printed, by inserting replacement pages. Page 13 is moved to become Page 17A, with minor amendments at its top and tail to make the material flow[77], and several pages in this section of the draft are labelled 'New Pages 8.7.86'. If we read this as 8 July 1986, this is after Saward ceased to be involved with television **Doctor Who** in any capacity (see Chapters 3, 4 and 5). This may, then, have been either a decision taken by Nathan-Turner as part of the 'softening' of the episode (see Intermission and Chapters 4 and 5), or a request made by the Bakers in order to have Part 13 fit more comfortably with **their** Part 14[78]. Alternatively, given that

---

[76] Holmes' draft has the Doctor react to the revelation with peculiar flippancy, saying 'Well, if he's really the twelfth Doctor perhaps I should start calling him the dockyard', continuing a running joke present in most episode of the series, where the Doctor insults the Valeyard by parodying his title as 'Railyard', 'Boatyard', 'Knacker's Yard', etc. This final example may be intended as payoff for the long-running wordplay, but it falls extremely flat on the page and it is hard to imagine any performer rescuing it.

[77] The bottom of Page 12 reads: 'Onto Page 14. No Page 13.'

[78] Although the Bakers have stated that they made no changes to Part 13 (Marson, 'Pip and Jane Baker'; Hearn, Marcus, 'Writing Who: Pip and Jane Baker', DWM #206) which they believed was entirely Holmes' work.

amendments were made to the rehearsal script, the need for the change may have emerged during rehearsals for the episode[79].

A final small change between (all) the scripted versions and this scene as performed is the loss of all but the first three words of the Doctor's exhortation to Glitz that 'We need him – if you want your money'. This is presumably on the grounds that Doctor can only suspect, but not know, that Glitz has been paid for attending the trial, and the confirmation of this to audience has been removed along with the original Scene 2.

Holmes' Scene 4 is included in the finished programme, with only incidental amendments, most of which seem like actorly interpretations (e.g. The Doctor says 'Quickly man, open it!' onscreen, rather than the scripted 'Then open it,' while The Inquisitor says 'Be silent!' rather than the scripted 'Silence girl!') The Inquisitor's exhortation to quiet is almost Holmes' last contribution to **Doctor Who**. None of the transmitted material set in the Matrix is his work. However, as noted above, Holmes' Scene 7, also set in the Trial Room, is presented almost wholly complete in the finished episode[80]. The only substantial cut is the loss of an exchange in which the Master thanks Melanie for calling him 'despicable' ('So many compliments... May I say you're a charming

---

[79] Having arranged a 'table read' of this draft while preparing this book, I can confirm that the sequence of events in this version of Scene 3 seemed peculiar to actors unfamiliar with the final draft, who commented on it without prompting.

[80] It is the scene beginning with The Inquisitor saying 'In all my experience, I have never before...' It's 16m 37s into the transmitted episode, chapter 5 on the DVD.

child?') and she responds by calling him a 'Beast!' before the Inquisitor again instructs her to be silent[81].

Holmes' Matrix scenes consist of four Telecines (numbered 2 to 5) and three numbered scenes – two set inside a Victorian hansom cab[82], and one that takes place in an 'Anteroom' within the Fantasy Factory itself.

Telecine 2[83] has the Doctor and Glitz already in the Matrix, where they discuss a piece of paper given to Glitz by the Master and now passed to the Doctor, which says the Valeyard is based in 'The Fantasy Factory, proprietor JJ Chambers'. The Doctor sniffs the air and says:

> 'Earth – somewhere at the turn of the nineteenth century. And that oily stagnance – a dock area [...] Yes. The fruit and spices of Old Indie. We could be in Liverpool or Marseille. But my guess is London.'

This is an interesting late example of Holmes' ability to sketch in an offscreen world in speech, and redolent of dialogue he gave Colin Baker's Doctor the year before in *The Two Doctors* ('There's nothing quite so evocative as one's sense of smell, is there?')[84]. Even more interestingly, on being told he is in a city Glitz is given

---

[81] This material was recorded, and is included as part of the 'Deleted Scenes' package on the *Trial of a Time Lord* DVD set.

[82] The Victorian setting of these scenes may be influenced by the 'Christmas Carol' structure of The Trial of a Time Lord, although it is worth noting that Dickens had been dead for nearly two decades by 1888.

[83] Telecine 1 was the earlier effects shot of the Time Lords' space station.

[84] *The Two Doctors* episode 1.

the line 'Population centres? [...] They had 'em in Andromeda once
– before the colonists' war'. This not only hints at a backstory
related to what transpired in Parts 1 to 4 that is never featured
onscreen, but may be thematically relevant, Victorian London being
the centre of a vast colonial empire. Following this grace note, the
Doctor and Glitz hail a cab and ask to be taken to the Fantasy
Factory.

Inside the cab (Scene 5) Glitz ponders its horse-drawn design, and
the Doctor says they are 'in a different world now, Glitz. And thirty
thousand years before your time.' In Part 1 the Ravolox scenes of
Parts 1 to 4 are said to take place 'Two billion years' after Peri's
time (c1985). This implies that Glitz, who has now after all been
revealed as an associate of the Master's, travelled in time as well as
space to reach Ravolox. It is also interesting in terms of backstory.
Holmes' 1975 story *The Ark in Space* featured characters from the
30th century and referenced wars in Andromeda[85], and it may be
that Holmes was positing a link between this story and one of his
biggest successes[86]. Alternatively, it could be an example of the

---

[85] *The Ark in Space* episodes 1, 4. **Doctor Who** fans have disputed
this dating, as **Doctor Who** fans are wont to do. (I am aware that
the 30th century is 1,000 years after the 20th century, not 30,000,
but the term resonates, and even without taking into account the
circumstances of this draft's composition Holmes' attitude to his
own continuity, even when utilising it, was frequently cavalier.)
[86] *The Ark in Space* episode 2 was seen by 13.6 million viewers, and
was the fifth most watched television programme the week of its
transmission, the highest placing ever achieved by 20th-century
Doctor Who. The serial has been praised by **Doctor Who**'s 21st-
century Executive Producers, Russell T Davies (2005-10) and Steven
Moffat (2010-17), as an outstanding example of the series, with
Moffat going so far as to write an introduction to a 2012 reprint of

self-recycling that his **Doctor Who** work had begun to exhibit by this point.

Scene 5 is brief, as is Telecine 3, in which the audience, but not the Doctor or Glitz, sees that the Cabman is the Valeyard. Scene 6 takes us back into the cab where, in response to Glitz asking how they can be in a different world when they 'just stepped through a door', The Doctor explains that in the Matrix 'the only logic is that there is no logic', a question and reply that survive and re-emerge in the transmitted episode's Telecine 2, with only the substitution of 'isn't any' for 'is no' – prompting in both instances an 'I knew this was a mistake' from Glitz.

Scene 6 ends with the Doctor realising the Cabman was the Valeyard, by belatedly recognising his voice, and opening the cab's door. This reveals that both the Cabman and his horses have disappeared. The cab then crashes, and although Glitz speculates that he has broken his neck, neither he nor the Doctor are injured. The Doctor then dismisses everything that has happened since they arrived in the matrix as 'The Valeyard's idea of a joke, I suppose'.

This sequence has interesting character aspects and good dialogue, but it is not hard to see why it was dispensed with. It would have been expensive (despite Holmes' script asking for it to be achieved 'using that old-fashioned thing, back projection'), and at its end

---

its novelisation detailing his admiration, and citing it as his favourite Tom Baker serial in his regular 'Production Notes' column in DWM #457. Davies, to give just one example, included it as part of a virtual TV festival he programmed for *The Guardian* in 2005. It exerts an observable influence on Davies' work within **Doctor Who**, especially his Doctors' tendency to make speeches on the topic of human achievement.

even its principal character dismisses it as a meaningless diversion. The 'Andromeda' references, and a lack of knowledge as to how Holmes intended to develop them further, are another convincing reason why Saward may have chosen to dispense with the evocative earlier material (of which more later).

In Telecine 4, the Doctor and Glitz abandon the wrecked cab to find themselves at their intended destination, the Fantasy Factory[87], which the Doctor recognises as being in 'Postern Row, George Yard'. They are approached by a character who identifies himself as 'Bencray' and who is described in the stage direction as:

> 'an old sea-dog with long white hair under some nondescript battered head-gear. He has a hoop-ring in his left ear to show he has sailed round the Horn. He has a wooden leg and a crutch.'

Bencray advises the Doctor and Glitz not to enter the Fantasy Factory and, implying it serves food, tells them 'That's a catsmeat gaffe [sic] in my opinion'. He then recommends the Doctor and Glitz purchase some of 'Bellamy's meat pies' instead, and notes that Bellamy's shop is near 'Sweeney Todd's barber's pole'. Holmes is mixing fact and fiction, and piling reference on top of reference here. Sweeney Todd, the murderous 'demon barber of Fleet Street' is, while assumed by many to be a historical figure, a fictional character[88]. Mrs Bellamy was Todd's accomplice, and her pies

---

[87] The factory's sign is here a 'brass plate'. In the rehearsal script it is a 'board'. The glowing, gloriously anachronistic neon sign seen in the transmitted episode is never mentioned in any draft.

[88] He is the anti-hero of *The String of Pearls: A Romance*, a serial published in 18 weekly parts, in *The People's Periodical and Family Library*, issues 7–24, 21 November 1846 to 20 March 1847.

contained the (human) flesh of his victims[89]. These references to cannibalism might be seen to be appropriate given that the Valeyard, who in this script is simply the 12th and final Doctor, is planning a kind of act of self-cannibalism in his attempt to steal the Doctor's remaining lives. (There is also perhaps a double reference: 'I think I could eat one of Bellamy's meat pies'[90] are the reputed last words of the British Prime William Pitt the Younger (1759-1806, in office 1783-1801, 1804-06).)

Bencray then talks about his 21st birthday, which he says was 'last year' (the Doctor picks up on the incongruity) and lists the guests at his 'Mafeking' of a party, including 'Polly Nichols, Annie Chapman, Long Liz Stride' and goes on to comment: 'they do say the gen'lman in the corner, enjoying hisself most hearty, was Royalty, sir.' The Doctor interprets this as a reference to 'the Duke of Clarence, no doubt?'[91] and Bencray confirms that this is who he meant. Bencray

---

[89] The eating of humans (by aliens) is a major aspect of Holmes' *The Two Doctors*. While this is not cannibalism per se, the story does use the iconography of the cannibalism-themed film *The Texas Chainsaw Massacre* (1974), and there is a brief conversation where it is stated that humans are a rare example of an intelligent species not routinely eating its own kind.

[90] There are many variations upon the phrase, which was reported by later Prime Minister, the Marquess of Roseberry (1847-1929, in office 1894-95) in his 1891 biography (Roseberry, Lord, *Pitt* p258). Roseberry claimed the anecdote had been passed to him by (yet another Prime Minister) Benjamin Disraeli (1804-81, in office 1868, 1874-80) who had heard it as a young MP from the man asked to bring the pie, who was later employed as a waiter at the House of Commons.

[91] Prince Albert Victor Christian Edward (1864–92), Duke of Clarence and Avondale from 1890 to his death, was the eldest son

then mentions that he is going to Sidcup because 'That's where me papers are, you see. Me documents. All in me diddy-box. When I get them I'll be all right.' This conversation is, oddly, a reference to Harold Pinter's *The Caretaker* (1960). Act One of this influential stage play contains the following exchange.

DAVIES

The weather's so blasted bloody awful, how can I get down to Sidcup in these shoes?

ASTON

Why do you want to get down to Sidcup?

DAVIES

I've got my papers there![92]

What Holmes may have meant by this, beyond tribute[93] and surrealism, is a mystery. (Sidcup, incidentally, is a suburban district of the London borough Bexley, but was in 1888, if not 1960, a village in Kent. Curiously, in 1986 the Doctor Who Appreciation Society was based there, and this additional reference may also be deliberate.)

In Scene 8 the Doctor and Glitz enter the Fantasy Factory, moving into an office described as 'a gloomy, dusty little place.' Intriguingly

---

of Edward, Prince of Wales and Princess Alexandra, the eldest grandson of Queen Victoria and throughout his short life the second in line to her crowns. He died in the influenza pandemic of the winter of 1891-92.

[92] Pinter, Harold, *The Caretaker*.

[93] *The Caretaker* being, in part, a play about two brothers which deals with uncertainties in identity.

the office is specified as having a 'Victorian style poster' on the wall:

> 'It shows the Valeyard, in Victorian dress, pointing like Kitchener in the [famous Great War] recruiting poster. The caption says, "DARE YOU TAKE MY CHALLENGE?"'

As in the finished episode the Doctor rings a bell for service, and here a panel in the office's wall is thrown back to reveal 'Bencray [...] But this Bencray has no ear-ring, no wooden leg, and is slightly better dressed. He does, however, have a left hook for a hand.'

Bencray enquires as to whether the Doctor would prefer 'trick or treat', and then 'puts a ball into a wheel and spins it. The ball falls into a slot.'[94] Bencray pronounces that, as a result of where the ball fell, 'You're playing murder. One of my favourites.' The Doctor informs Bencray he is aware that the women whose names he was given outside were murdered by Jack the Ripper[95], which leads Bencray to conclude they have been talking to his brother. He becomes furious at the idea that the other Bencray claims to be 21,

---

[94] Although the exact meaning this piece of 'business' is unclear from the text, it is possible the reference is to a roulette wheel.

[95] 'Jack the Ripper' is the name given to whoever committed the unsolved murders of (a minimum of) five prostitutes in London's Whitechapel between late August and early November 1888. 'Jack' was never successfully identified, and several hundred 'solutions' to the case have been proposed by practitioners of the pseudo-social science of 'ripperology'. The name 'Jack the Ripper', originally bestowed by contemporary press reports has lived on, and the term 'ripper' has subsequently been frequently applied by the media to other British serial killers of women, e.g. Peter Sutcliffe, Steven James Wright.

when in fact he is 32[96]. The Doctor notes that the other Bencray's reference to Mafeking was also anachronistic[97], to which Bencray responds:

> 'I'm always telling 'em they should take more care with the scripts. But do they listen? They do not! As long as it ends happily with the death of the challengers, that's all they bother about!'

Saward reports that Holmes' was upset by Powell's criticisms of the scripts for Parts 1 to 4, and it is hard not to interpret this, and some other elements of this draft, in light of this knowledge.

Following this metafictional statement, Bencray gets Glitz to sign a consent form absolving the Fantasy Factory of responsibility should he die within it, and the Doctor to sign another ('You're one of these multi-lifers, I see. That's more paperwork for me, you know,' he comments) which means that if and when the Doctor loses the game of 'murder', Mr JJ Chambers 'collects the rest of your

---

[96] The joke, of course, being that the other Bencray is specified as 'old'.

[97] Taking place on 17 May 1900, the relief of Mafeking was a militarily insignificant event in the Second Boer War. It was nevertheless a huge boost to British war morale and coined the short-lived verb, to 'mafek' or 'maffik' meaning to party or celebrate, which referenced the wild celebrations in the UK when news of the siege's lifting was received. This was 12 years after the Whitechapel murders, making Bencray's reference a deliberate anachronism on Holmes' part. Intriguingly, describing something as happening 'shortly before Mafeking was relieved' is an idiom frequently invoked by Michael Grade, and again the reference may be deliberate.

existences'[98]. Bencray notes that the Doctor cannot win because 'we write the scripts'[99]. The Doctor and Glitz then leave Bencray's office through a different door from the one they entered by.

Telecine 5 is the final scene of the script. The Doctor and Glitz emerge back onto the streets of London, and almost immediately hear 'terrible anguished screams'. Glitz asks 'What's that?' and the Doctor responds 'Scene one', in yet another metafictional touch[100]. The Doctor rushes to help whoever it is being attacked, but Glitz is reluctant. Finding that the screams are coming from inside a building, the Doctor looks through a window and sees a murder being committed. He attempts entry, but the door is barred. He rushes around the back of the building to try and find another door, but is stopped by two 'toffs'. They are identified in stage directions, but not dialogue, as 'The Duke of Clarence and his friend J Stephens.' The Duke unsheathes a swordstick and accuses the Doctor of being Jack the Ripper. This the Doctor denies, but the Duke points out that the Doctor's clothes are covered in blood. The Doctor looks down, and they suddenly are. Threatening to send him 'back to Hades', the Duke lunges at the Doctor, who steps aside, tripping over a low wall and falling into 'the black, oily water of a wharf'. The 'toffs' resolve to let the Doctor drown, but then there is another burst of screaming from the building. Realising

---

[98] The prize for winning is 'a million golden guineas', which can hardly be considered an equitable stake.
[99] It is unclear to whom this plural pronoun refers, and in the absence of a Holmes version of Part 14, clarity can never be achieved.
[100] As the preantepenultimate page of the script, and the first line of its final scene, this would almost certainly have formed the beginning – 'Scene One' – of any Part 14 Homes had lived to write.

that they have attacked and possibly killed the wrong man, the Duke and Stephens run away. The Doctor's motionless body lies in the water as the fleeing Duke incongruously shouts 'A horse! A horse! My kingdom for a horse!'[101]

What are we make of this excised and, at best, heavily rewritten material? Saward has noted that he 'rewrote the second half to make it fit for what I wanted for the last part', and on another occasion that he 'rewrote episode 13 so I could go on to write episode 14, because what Bob had intended was different to what I would do.'[102]

Where **did** Holmes intend to go with the story? We just don't know. It is not unreasonable to intuit that that the details removed by Saward represent clues to Holmes' intentions from which Saward was unable to extrapolate a conclusion of his own[103]. The references to Andromeda and the colonists' wars link the second half of Holmes' Part 13 both to Parts 1 to 4, and to the lengthy

---

[101] Quoting Act V scene 4 of Shakespeare's *Richard III* (1592), in which an earlier royal Duke of Clarence appears (though he does not speak the lines).

[102] Saward, Part 13 DVD commentary. It might reasonably be thought that this explanation does not wholly mesh with Saward's also frequently stated desire to honour Holmes' intentions for the serial.

[103] In the 1980s, writers for **Doctor Who** usually had to submit at least one draft of a detailed outline before being commissioned to write a script for the series. It is worth noting that Holmes seemingly did not have to do this in this case, and apparently didn't discuss much of the detail with the Script Editor; Saward's trust in his mentor's demonstrable ability to write for **Doctor Who** having problematic consequences when his health failed.

discussion of Ravolox and the Time Lords in Scene 3, which was written by Homes and is preserved in the finished episode. It seems likely that this, something that neither Saward's Part 14 nor Pip and Jane Baker's replacement refer to, is relevant to Holmes' intentions.

There are other questions that this script prompts. What is Bencray's function within the story?[104] Are there really two of him? What is his 'diddy box' and what are the 'papers' within it? Is Bencray perhaps the Master in disguise? That question may, on the surface, seem fatuous, but the Master is historically a character who indulges in implausible disguises, and we know both that Holmes was aware of this, and that Holmes's intention was for the Master to emerge as the ultimate villain of the story. Perhaps more significantly, Davies in *The Caretaker*, the character who speaks about Sidcup, is living under an assumed identity.

It is notable that the Valeyard hardly features in the Matrix sections of Holmes's Part 13. While the Valeyard does not appear onscreen after he exits the courtroom in the transmitted Part 13, Saward does give him dialogue in voiceover during the episode's cliffhanger, and earlier scenes frequently feature his disembodied, mocking laughter. These things combine to give the character considerable 'presence' in the second half of the episode despite his not appearing in shot[105]. The Valeyard's absence from Holmes' draft can be seen as a process of moving the character to one side,

---

[104] Is he Jack the Ripper? He is the only available suspect in the fiction within the fiction, assuming he isn't an avatar for another character.
[105] A shot of the Valeyard emerging outside the Fantasy Factory was recorded for Part 13 but cut in editing.

so that the Master can assume the central antagonistic role in Holmes' conception of Part 14. (In this context, the Master's line to the Inquisitor, and the last line of Robert Holmes dialogue to appear in **Doctor Who**, 'What more could a renegade wish for?' seems more than merely rhetorical, which is how it presents in the finished story.)

Holmes' own *The Deadly Assassin* (1976), which introduced the concept of the Time Lords' virtual-reality Matrix, devotes almost its entire third episode to a battle in the Matrix between the Doctor and an adversary, Chancellor Goth, who turns out to be a puppet of the Master's. Had the intention to have the Master as the serial's ultimate villain played out by having the Valeyard also turn out to be subordinate to the Master in some way, then the resemblance between the two stories, already considerable, would be even more striking. *The Deadly Assassin* is also, like Holmes's Part 13 and Saward's Part 14, about a desperate Time Lord in his last incarnation attempting to continue his own life. In the earlier story, that Time Lord was the Master, not a future Doctor. This makes it also peculiar that, despite the Valeyard's aim and motivation in Holmes' Part 13 and Saward's Part 14 being **exactly the same** as the Master's in *The Deadly Assassin*, **and** the presence of the Master in *The Trial of a Time Lord*, **and** the two stories sharing a writer, no draft of either of the final two episodes refers to the irony of the Doctor being reduced to the Master's level, of him emulating one of his enemy's previous plans.

Given this, is it possible, considering the self-plagiarism already on display, that Holmes' version would have seen the Master revealed as himself planning to steal the Doctor's lives, with the Valeyard merely his pawn? Saward has indicated that Holmes intended for

Part 14's final scene to be the Doctor and the Master trapped in a physical struggle, reminiscent of Sherlock Holmes and Professor Moriarty at the conclusion of Arthur Conan Doyle's 'The Final Problem' (1893), in which the two fight and then pitch over a waterfall seemingly to mutual death. This is something that forces us to wonder what the Valeyard would have been doing at this point in Holmes' version. Has he been killed by the Master? Maybe in Holmes's conception, the Valeyard would ultimately revert to type, i.e. realise that he is essentially the Doctor, and aid his earlier incarnation in defeating the Master. He might do this, perhaps, after discovering both that he is not going to receive the extension of life that he was promised and the scale of what the Master is prepared to do in order to prolong his own – assuming that reality-destroying Time Vent in Saward's Part 14 was part of the 'vague outline' he had agreed with Holmes. (If it wasn't, it's hard to see what this outline, however vague, could have contained.)

Is it possible that, given the already inherently paradoxical nature of the final two episodes and the references to colonists' wars and widespread destruction in Andromeda as well as the devastation of Earth seen in Parts 1 to 4, that Holmes's script would present an opportunity to reverse or undo the High Council's attack on the latter, and possibly the former too? (The devastated Earth of Part 1, with its ruined tube station and surviving 19th and 20th-century books, seems to be a planet destroyed in the late 20th century, not 30,000[106] or 2,000,000,000[107] years after 1986.)

---

[106] As in this draft of Part 13.

[107] The implication of taking the Doctor's conclusion in Part 1 that he and Peri are 'two billion years' after her time in context with all

This tempting and somewhat wild (albeit textually-prompted) speculation does not take much account of this script's other main difference from the transmitted Part 13, Holmes' extensive use of iconography and historical information related to the 'Whitechapel Murders' of 1888, the so-called 'Jack the Ripper' case. The imminence of the centenary of the these killings may have prompted Holmes to write his Part 13, and it is possible he was aware of David Wickes' **Jack the Ripper** series for Thames Television (1988), which was already in production[108]. (Wickes, like Holmes, had worked for Philip Hinchcliffe in BBC Drama in 1976-78.) However, the preceding decade had seen a flurry of interest in the unsolved Ripper case, mostly due to Stephen Knight's hugely successful 1976 book *Jack the Ripper: The Final Solution*, which was not only massively influential in its day, but continues to be so – despite the book's main source, Joseph Gorman, later admitting that he had hoaxed Knight, Knight's many errors of basic fact (e.g., a building key to his theory had been demolished before 1888) and his book's dependence on irrelevant coincidences as evidence (e.g. that two characters in his story were Danish).

---

versions of Part 13's statement that the Time Lords destroyed Earth 'centuries' (rather than millennia) before the Doctor's trial.

[108] Eventually produced and screened as an expensive, all-film co-production with US Network CBS and starring the bona fide film star and recent Oscar winner Michael Caine, the series was already in development as a mid-budget VT series starring Barry Foster. This version made it to studio before being cancelled during shooting, and scenes from the aborted production exist. It's a rather splendid coincidence that both productions feature Ken Bones, who in *The Time of the Doctor* (2013) would play the Time Lord responsible for extending the Doctor's life beyond 13 incarnations.

Gorman had claimed to be the illegitimate son of the painter Walter Sickert and a woman called Alice Cook, herself the daughter of an illegal marriage between an Anne Cook, who was one of Sickert's models, and Queen Victoria's grandson Prince Albert Victor. The Ripper murders were, by this account, the killings of friends and associates of Gorman's grandmother, conducted on the orders of a Masonic conspiracy, in order to cover up the existence of her daughter, his mother. Gorman's first claim is, as he later acknowledged, demonstrably false, and while the latter two claims cannot be absolutely demonstrated to be untrue there is no evidence at all that they are anything other than the fantasy Gorman admitted they were. Gorman was probably building his own hoax on an article by Dr Thomas Stowell entitled 'Jack the Ripper: A Solution?' which appeared in the November 1970 issue of *The Criminologist*[109]. Stowell was the first writer to implicate Prince Albert Victor in the Ripper case, implying rather than stating that the Prince himself had committed the murders. (The Prince's demonstrable attendance at dated public events when some of the murders were committed[110] has prompted later extrapolated theories that they were performed on his behalf, but not by him in person.)

---

[109] This was not, as is sometimes implied, an academic journal, but effectively a semi-professional quarterly fanzine which combined articles on real-life crime and crime fiction. It ran from 1967-98 and was edited by the crime fiction author Nigel Morland.

[110] E.g. the Court Circular for 20 September 1888 records the Prince's attendance at a dinner with foreign dignitaries in front of dozens of witnesses in Scotland. This was the night Elizabeth Stride and Catherine Eddowes were murdered.

The Prince, of course, features as a character in the final scene of Holmes' Part 13, where he is presented, at least by his own account, as hunting Jack the Ripper, rather than portrayed as a suspect in (the Valeyard's Matrix recreation of) the Whitechapel murders[111]. That the screams of one of the Ripper's victims are heard offscreen as the Prince and his companion[112] struggle with the Doctor also suggests that Holmes did not intend to 'finger' the Prince as the Ripper, even in a fiction-within-a-fiction. The script does, though, through Bencray's earlier comments, perpetuate the unevidenced claim, originated by Stowell in 1970, that the Prince was known to the Whitechapel murderer's victims[113].

---

[111] The Prince was not yet Duke of Clarence, as Holmes' script refers to him, at the time of the Whitechapel murders, being granted this title by his grandmother in 1890. This is an error often made in even ostensibly serious books about the Whitechapel murders, but may here reflect Holmes' general, and the episode's specific, interest in anachronism as dramatic furniture.

[112] The Duke's companion is named 'Stephens' in stage directions, and the Duke at one point calls him 'Jim'. James Kenneth Stephen (no 's') (1859-92) was a barrister, minor English poet, first cousin to Virginia Woolf and a Cambridge contemporary of the Prince. A head injury in 1886 is blamed for his exponentially increasingly odd public behaviour from that year, and his later long-term hospitalisation and early death at the age of 33. He too is an occasional 'Ripper' suspect, although he was publicly lecturing at Cambridge on the dates of at least some of the murders.

[113] This claim is seemingly effected by reading back from the Prince being named in non-UK newspapers as being 'mixed up' in the Cleveland Street scandal of 1889, in which a male brothel was discovered and closed down by police. There is no direct evidence of the Prince's involvement in **this** scandal either, but he was at least connected to it in contemporary reports, rather than nearly a

Almost exactly 10 years before, at the height of the interest in Knight's book, Holmes had written *The Talons of Weng-Chiang* (1977) a **Doctor Who** serial that mentions 'Jolly Jack... the Ripper', and deals in part with the abduction and murder of young women, at least one of whom is implied to be a prostitute. *Talons*, though, presents a version of the story which, while unable to wholly shed the inherent misogyny of the premise, uses science-fiction elements to make it less overt, and does not feature any specific facts or theories related to the Whitechapel murders[114].

This, as we've already seen, is very much not the case with Holmes's Part 13, and there are further occasions where facts related to the Whitechapel murders are used in the script. For example, the Fantasy Factory is said to be in George Yard. George Yard was the location where the body of Martha Tabram, a Whitechapel prostitute murdered on 7 August 1888, was found. Tabram is sometimes included in lists of Jack the Ripper's victims. Other lists discount her, arguing that the manner of her death – 37

---

century later, and it was certainly the case that the brothel was used by society figures. These included Lord Arthur Somerset, head of the Prince's father's stables, who left Britain to avoid being charged in relation to attending the brothel, dying in Paris in 1926. It is something of a gift to those constructing Jack the Ripper conspiracies that the Cleveland Street brothel was closed down by Frederick Abberline (1843-1929), the Metropolitan Police detective who investigated the Whitechapel murders.

[114] The borrowings from *The Krotons* (1969) and *The Ribos Operation* in Holmes's scripts for Parts 1 to 4, and from *The Deadly Assassin* and *The Talons of Weng-Chiang* here, might be taken to imply merit in Nathan-Turner's reluctance to bring back old **Doctor Who** writers, believing they would repeat themselves due to being, in his own phrase, 'Who-ed out'.

stab wounds, but no slashing at the throat or genital mutilation – means the unfortunate woman, while brutally murdered, was the victim of another killer, one unconnected with the 'Ripper' assumed to be responsible for the so-called 'canonical five' victims – the three women who Holmes has Bencray mention to the Doctor, plus Catherine Eddowes and Mary Jane Kelly.

It would have been striking in itself to have had the names of three of the Ripper's real victims said aloud in a **Doctor Who** story, overtly linking real life tragedy with television fantasy. Yet more surprising is Holmes' script's request that the Ripper, his knife and profile be depicted as he commits one of his murders onscreen, in a sequence which, by showing a murder inside a locked building, seems to deliberately invoke the death of Mary Jane Kelly[115]:

> 'Inside, on the far wall, a gas-lit shadow with a knife is crouched, its arm slashing **and slashing again**. The cries have bubbled away.'

Here we have the writer asking for a scene in which a serial killer murders and mutilates a young woman with a knife, watched through a window by Doctor Who himself. You don't have to be Mary Whitehouse to feel this is not a matter for a space adventure serial destined to be transmitted at 5:20pm.

---

[115] Unlike the other four 'canonical' Ripper victims, Mary Jane Kelly's body was found indoors, on the bed on which she was murdered. Kelly is usually considered the Ripper's last victim. If Martha Tabram is added to the list of those killed by him, she would be the first, and it might be relevant that these scenes span from the beginning of the Ripper murders to their end.

There is, it has to be acknowledged, something unsettling about Holmes' script. The fixation with death and its imagery is pronounced, even if the reader is unaware that Holmes would not live to see the script enter production. Glitz arrives in a coffin, serial murder is discussed and even seen, and the Doctor appears to die during the cliffhanger, shortly after he discovers he is covered in what appears to be the blood of a prostitute whose terrible murder he has just witnessed. Both Glitz and the Doctor are induced to sign forms absolving others of responsibility for their deaths, and Bencray notes that all the audience really wants is to see characters die. Even the frequent use of the word 'murder', rarely heard in **Doctor Who**, adds to the grim atmosphere.

I am not temperamentally inclined to biographical readings of texts, but it is very hard to not see much of this script, excellent though it often is, as the work of the dying man we know it to be. These factors also surely make the script unsuitable for the early evening slot in which it was due to be transmitted, maybe even unsuitable as an instalment of the programme of which it was meant to be a key part. Had the script as written been shot, the resultant episode would certainly have been the most overtly horrific episode of **Doctor Who** made up to that point – which might be seen as an odd thing for a production team who had been instructed to tone down the violence in the series to make. It may have been this unsuitability, in both senses, and perhaps a lack of any desire to write follow-up scenes on the same topic himself, that prompted Saward to completely remove Holmes' Jack the Ripper elements from the episode.

There is, of course, another obvious issue: Saward's seeming lack of knowledge as to how Holmes intended to resolve these plot strands. It may also simply be that he was unable to work out how to progress from Holmes's own draft, and that any secondary material he had related to the planned climax was insufficiently detailed to help. He had visited Holmes in hospital and found him debilitated to the point where he could not communicate effectively, or even recognise close friends and family[116].

Again, all we can do is speculate as to what Holmes would have done. Are these scenes, like many in *The Deadly Assassin*, simply horrific surrealism, with no function beyond the symbolic, or did Holmes plan to posit a 'solution' to the Jack the Ripper 'mystery'[117]? If so, did he intend to propose one that could be read across into 'real life', as David Wickes' 1988 drama would, or would it be a science-fictional explanation that could only 'make sense' within the context of **Doctor Who**[118]? Was Holmes' take on the material interrogative, as Alan Moore's would later be[119], or was he

---

[116] While the impossibility of asking the ailing writer what he had intended to write next is far from the most important or most distressing aspect of Holmes' illness and incapacitation, it was nevertheless the case.

[117] It is worth noting that in all versions of *The Trial of a Time Lord*, the Valeyard is a part of an establishment conspiracy to cover up a crime committed by Gallifrey's ruling class. This thematic resonance with much 'ripperology' is not inappropriate, perhaps the only aspect of this section of the script that isn't.

[118] *Wolf in the Fold*, a 1967 **Star Trek** episode by Robert Bloch (the author of the novel *Psycho* (1959)) posits that 'Jack' was an alien entity that possesses people and compels them to commit murder, although it at least has the decency to not present this as a 'credible' solution to the identity of the real-life killer.

[119] *From Hell* (1999, originally serialised 1988-96), a graphic novel by Alan Moore and Eddie Campbell initially seems to offer a

presenting his own solution to the mystery of Jack the Ripper's identity as Wickes was about to? Is the Doctor accused of being Jack the Ripper because the Valeyard, who is also the Doctor, was himself to be revealed as Jack the Ripper in Part 14[120]?

Nobody knows.

Given the extreme difficulty in extrapolating what Holmes wanted, intended or meant by the latter half of his final **Doctor Who** episode – even now, and in a situation considerably less stressful than that Saward faced in 1986 – judicious use of Occam's razor suggests that this, combined with the material's excessive unpleasantness (as distinct from 'darkness') is the most significant reason for the scale of the rewrite. It is certainly the most understandable.

Having looked at the original draft, and conjectured as to reasons why such a radical rewrite was deemed necessary, in our next chapter we'll look at the transmitted version of the programme, with occasional reference to its final rehearsal script, to further examine how Saward reshaped the episode during his own redrafting.

---

fictional explanation for the Whitechapel murders, but then unwinds its own theories, becoming about the nature of conspiracy theory in general, as well as the Ripper 'industry' specifically. It is unreservedly recommended, although its 2001 film adaptation is not.

[120] That the Valeyard was Jack the Ripper is the basis of the 1998 **Doctor Who** novel *Matrix*, co-written by Mike Tucker, who was a visual effects assistant on *The Trial of a Time Lord*, although there has never been any suggestion that Tucker saw Holmes' first draft script.

CHAPTER 3: PART 13 BY ROBERT HOLMES (AND ERIC SAWARD, UNCREDITED)

We've already established that the first to fourth and sixth scenes, and an initial effects Telecine, from Holmes's script were presented substantially unaltered in the final version of Part 13. Between them, they account for roughly half of the final episode. The other half, which is not by Holmes, consists of scenes which occur after the Doctor and Glitz go through the Seventh Door, and all but one of them of is set inside the Matrix.

Saward revised Part 13 in his capacity as **Doctor Who**'s Script Editor, and therefore there are no records of exactly when he began or completed his work on it, or when he moved onto writing his version of Part 14. His work on Part 13, though, must have been completed before he resigned from the BBC on 13 April 1986. Saward had been under pressure for at least a year, the production team had literally written off as many scripts as they'd accepted for the 1986 series of **Doctor Who**, and Holmes' illness had taken a huge emotional toll on the younger writer:

> 'I said ultimately to John... "I feel I can't serve this any more, I've given so much to it already." John was sort of understanding, I think he was also terrified that he might be left to finish the series on his own, which he ultimately was.'

Before resigning, though, he spent some time working on **Doctor Who** from home, to see if matters improved:

> 'I went home for a fortnight as a Script Editor. I think John was hoping I'd recover and feel better about things, and I didn't, and I came back and instead of stepping calmly into

an office I just walked back into another sea of chaos, and problems and difficulties.'

Saward resigned as **Doctor Who**'s Script Editor, but continued to work on Part 14 in his new capacity as a freelance writer. Saward's unanticipated departure meant that, during this period, Nathan-Turner did 'double duty' serving as both Script Editor and Producer on **Doctor Who**, having been informed in a brief meeting with Jonathan Powell that there were no staff script editors available to take Saward's place at such short notice, and that he would have to make do[121].

Some small work was undertaken on Part 13's script after Saward's departure, almost entirely to help link the beginning of Part 13 to the end of Part 12, which had not been delivered when he

---

[121] This strongly echoes Powell's later recollection that there was no one else available to produce **Doctor Who** in 1985. By 1986, while Script Editor was nominally a staff position, there were several freelancers working in the job as contractors, as indeed Saward had, so what was to stop Nathan-Turner hiring another, other than Powell's instruction not to? In a similar gap between permanent editors five years before, Antony Root had been rotated on to **Doctor Who** in the short term, and it was not unusual for staff Script Editors to be moved onto a second series between runs of their main programme, e.g. Chris Boucher's work on the second half of the 1980 series of **Shoestring** (1979-80) between the third and fourth series of **Blake's 7**. It may be that Powell was not interested in solving **Doctor Who**'s problems, as his comments elsewhere indicate. It may also be speculated that no one wished to work on what was now perceived as a sinking ship, or that the often divisive Nathan-Turner did not have good enough relations with any available staff member.

resigned[122]. Something in relation to these minor additions is worthy of comment. The transmitted Part 13 has the Valeyard and the Inquisitor discuss the additional charge of genocide, which has been sprung on the Doctor as the cliffhanger to Part 12, following his presentation of his own evidence. While this discussion is brief, the matter will be returned to in the transmitted Part 14. This plot development has been much criticised, with the illogical nature of the Doctor being charged mid-case for a crime that he has not committed except in a hypothetical future drawing particular scorn.

While paradoxical, this is not as illogical as it seems. It obviously makes little sense from a human perspective, but the Time Lords are a trans-temporal species, and we will shortly discover that two people in the courtroom are in fact the same person at different points in his life. A civilisation capable of both time travel and accessing hypothetical futures may very well have legal procedures for dealing with crimes before they occur, by executing the future criminal in order to prevent the offence being committed. If anything, this interestingly bizarre idea makes more sense as a demonstration of how Time Lord jurisprudence could function, than the rest of the serial's presentation of it as a parody of courtroom drama about English law[123].

---

[122] Pip Baker remembers working with Saward only on Part 9, the first of the four episodes of the Vervoid story (Hearn, 'Writing Who').

[123] The two Time Lord trials seen in Episode 10 of *The War Games* are more satisfyingly abstract. There are charges, but both the War Lord and the Doctor defend themselves by offering a counter-thesis to that provided by the tripartite panel who seem to be prosecutor, judge, jury and executioner, and the black space with screens controlled by 'thought channels' in which they take place is more

The one non-Matrix **and** non-Holmes scene in the transmitted Part 13 is a replacement Scene 5, and there is some ambiguity as to its author. The scene, which takes place in the courtroom, sees the Inquisitor asking the Master how much of the evidence against the Doctor had been contrived by the Valeyard, and the Master giving an ambiguous answer. The Inquisitor presses him as to whether Peri, who the court saw die as part of the evidence relayed during Part 8, is really dead or not, and the Master tells her that Peri is alive, and is now Yrcanos' Queen[124].

This scene, which is neither from Holmes' draft nor modelled on anything from it, has its origins in a query from Colin Baker to the series' production team. Seeking clarity as to which sections of the Doctor's experiences on Thoros Beta, as seen in Parts 5 to 8, were invented by the Valeyard and which really happened[125], Baker asked Saward if Peri's death was part of the Valeyard's faked evidence or not, reasoning that if it were not, she could still be alive:

> 'I said "Did that happen? Was that a Matrix lie? Does the Doctor know? What's the story Eric? We need to explain it."

---

visually arresting than the large, expensive but essentially dull courtroom set used throughout the 1986 series.

[124] Those who object to the idea of Peri as a warrior queen are invited to take the Master's description 'She is a queen, set up on high by that warmongering fool Yrcanos,' less literally than the Inquisitor does when relaying the information to the Doctor in the transmitted Part 14.

[125] Those so inclined can discover Baker finally being offered this clarity in real time by writer Philip Martin on their shared DVD commentary track for Parts 5 to 8.

Eric came back with one line from Lynda Bellingham saying she went off with Yrcanos and married [him].'

[Colin Baker]

By Baker's account, Saward then, in his capacity as Script Editor, wrote this scene in order to clarify matters, at some point before 13 April. However, Nathan-Turner says he must take responsibility for including a scene negating Peri's death as 'part and parcel of attempting to leave our audience with a degree of safety this time,' and adds that the decision to do so 'was mine and mine alone'[126]. (This, of course, does not necessarily negate the possibility of the idea being suggested by Baker's questions, and of the dialogue answering that question being written by Saward; it merely means that Nathan-Turner decided Saward should write something that answered Baker's question.) The scene is included in the original pagination of the final script for Part 13, and is not on inserted, replacement or renumbered pages. Additionally, Saward does not call out the sequence as being scripted by anyone else on his solo DVD commentary for the episode. Nevertheless, the possibility of it being written by Nathan-Turner after Saward's departure can't be discounted either[127].

---

[126] Nathan-Turner, John, 'This Must be the Place I Waited Years to Leave', DWM #245.

[127] There is an awkwardness to the opening dialogue, largely cut from the transmitted episode, that suggests a non-writer 'making do'. The few relevant sentences in the scene could easily have been interpolated into Holmes' original Scene 6, which is indeed what the Bakers do with the material in their novelisation. A more impactful approach to the companion issue in these episodes would have been to have the Master whisk Peri away from her fate

Saward's version of the Matrix scenes are both very different, and clearly derived, from the equivalent section of Holmes' draft[128]. Holmes' Jack the Ripper nightmare is replaced by a very different, but still Victorian, fantasy world largely, if perhaps superficially, drawn from the work of Charles Dickens.

The Doctor and Glitz enter separately, rather than together, with the Doctor appearing first and being attacked by a pair of gnarled hands that reach out of a barrel to strangle him, before Glitz arrives and disrupts the attack. As in Holmes' draft, he gives the Doctor a note from the Master informing him that the Valeyard's base is at 'The Fantasy Factory, proprietor JJ Chambers'[129], but rather than having to take a cab there, it turns out they are already outside it.

---

on Thoros Beta order to testify, instead of Mel. The arrival of the presumed dead Peri in the court would have provided a more effective cliffhanger to Part 12, and as Parts 13 to 14 were recorded first, Nicola Bryant's presence could have been easily hidden, while it would have been a nice dramatic irony for the Master to save her when the Doctor had failed so to do. But it does seem she was supposed to die, until Colin Baker intervened.

[128] For the structure of the finished episode, please see Appendix 2: Scene Breakdowns (Part 13). As the transmitted programme is available on DVD, this chapter will not devote more space to describing the order of events in this version than is strictly necessary.

[129] The phrase is spoken onscreen by Glitz and in the script by the Doctor, almost the only dialogue after the Doctor enters the Matrix to survive the redrafting without any alteration at all. One wonders if Saward inserted the delay between the Doctor's arrival and Glitz's to imply that this is when Glitz is given the message by the Master.

In the place of the Bencray brothers, the Doctor and Glitz meet two Mr Popplewicks, one junior and one senior. Both Popplewicks are encountered inside the Fantasy Factory and both seem to be employees of 'Mr JJ Chambers'. (The older Bencray, met in the street outside the factory in Holmes' draft, is a sailor who criticises the Fantasy Factory.) Popplewick's name recalls Dickens' *The Pickwick Papers* (1836)[130] although the character was conceived by Saward as 'the ultimate of bureaucrats' and is described as 'Dressed in late Victorian clerk's attire... A thin, angular man in his mid-forties. Everything about him is sour – including his breath', making him the antithesis of the warm-hearted and overweight Pickwick. This surely deliberate contrast was later muddied when rotund actor Geoffrey Hughes was cast, after director Chris Clough found he could think of no one suitable for the part who also fitted the description, and decided to look for the opposite sort of actor instead, in the process inverting a deliberate inversion[131].

The duplicate Popplewicks provide the same surreal note as the duplicate Bencrays, and the Senior Mr Popplewick's function, in getting the Doctor and Glitz to sign disclaimers, is identical to the second Bencray's. The dialogue of the scenes featuring the two Mr Popplewicks is all new, however. In place of Holmes' metafictional worrying, references to Jack the Ripper conspiracy theories and nods to Pinter and penny dreadfuls come a series of comments on, and jokes about, bureaucracy, with the Junior Mr Popplewick forbidden to expect visitors, even those who are known to the

---

[130] *The Pickwick Papers* is not, of course, a Victorian novel.
[131] There can, though, be no complaints about Hughes' performance in the role, which is excellent.

Senior Mr Popplewick to be arriving shortly, and it being made clear that if he were 'tipped the nod' for his own convenience, his pride would be hurt. While it would be easy to see these sequences as originating in Saward's frustrations with BBC procedures, perhaps with particular reference to the **Doctor Who** production office, frustration with bureaucracy is a key theme of Dicken's later work, most celebrated in the portrayal of the Circumlocution Office in *Little Dorrit* (1857, originally serialised 1855-7).

The final script for the episode assumes that the Popplewicks' offices will be studio sets, and suggests 'the lounge of the space ship redressed' as a cost-saving measure – i.e. the lounge of the *Hyperion III*, a set required for Parts 9 to 12 which formed part of the same production (the aforementioned '7C') as Parts 13 and 14. However, it was decided that the non-courtroom sections of Parts 9 to 12 would be recorded after all work on Parts 13 and 14 had been completed. This would mean that the set would not yet be available. If it were, it would be being 'reused' before its primary use, making this a kind of real-life paradox. However, it was decided to record these scenes on location when Chris Clough's choice of the Gladstone Pottery Museum for the Fantasy Factory's exteriors proved to have a period office suitable for use. Dialogue for the Doctor in which he comments on the incongruity Saward had anticipated ('The combination is a bit odd. Hi-tech vistani alloy walls cocooning what appears to be rather a crusty Victorian clerk. All very anachronistic.') was deleted before recording[132].

---

[132] It is preserved in the Bakers' novelisation, however, a further indication that they were working from an earlier draft of the script when writing the book (Baker and Baker, *The Ultimate Foe* p47).

In the episode's final scene, the Doctor leaves Popplewick's office to find himself alone on a beach. He argues with the Valeyard's disembodied voice before being dragged into the ground by grasping hands resembling those that attacked him in the alleyway outside the Fantasy Factory[133].

Saward's Matrix scenes are noticeably 'lighter' than Holmes's. While dramatic, and retaining the surrealism of Holmes' submission, they lack the queasiness and frequent invocation of real-life murders, the sharp knives and onscreen blood, of the first draft. Dickens is perceived as a family-friendly writer, even given the extremes often present in his work, and his novels are often adapted for children's or family television. Saward's draft and the final episode reflect that. Dickens is also, need it be said, the author of *A Christmas Carol*, the novella which inspired *The Trial of a Time Lord*'s past-present-future structure, which makes references to his work here more appropriate than a list of facts about Jack the Ripper.

It has to be said that Saward's rewrite of Part 13 is both a strong episode of **Doctor Who** in its own right, and an impressive reworking of Holmes' material. It honours the essence of Holmes' draft, and keeps many of its fascinations, while dispensing with material that the production team could not stage effectively, may not have considered suitable, or could not divine the purpose of. It also effectively sets the stage for Saward's conclusion to the series.

---

[133] **Doctor Who** fans with a liking for retroactive continuity might like to assume that they are imported examples of the Skarosian 'hand mines' introduced in *The Magician's Apprentice* (2015).

But that conclusion, like Holmes' own, was never to reach the screen.

Saward's five-year tenure on **Doctor Who** ends with the Doctor being drowned in sand. It is grimly interesting, given the circumstances of the script's revision and what transpired after its completion, that it evokes a classic symbol of depression in its final moment.

This image, if not the Doctor's words[134], were Saward's last transmitted work on **Doctor Who**. He delivered his script for Part 14 and Nathan-Turner, in his capacity as Script Editor and Producer, gave notes. A series of phone calls and a flurry of correspondence between the two men followed, as they disagreed over elements of the finale.

On 4 June 1986, Saward realised that there was no compromise between his teleplay as it stood and Nathan-Turner's notes on it which both of them would accept. Worried that Nathan-Turner would carry out a final draft of the script himself, in the process implementing changes over which they had disagreed, Saward withdrew permission for his script for Part 14 to be used and ceased all communication with the **Doctor Who** production office.

---

[134] The Doctor's final line of the episode is a 'Noooooooooo!' delivered in extreme close-up. Nathan-Turner had a 'favour the Doctor' policy when it came to episode endings. 13 of the 14 episodes of *The Trial of a Time Lord* end with a close-up of the Doctor.

INTERMISSION: WHO IS THE VALEYARD

In Holmes' draft of Part 13, the Valeyard's identity is straightforward. But it would not remain so for long.

> MASTER
>
> Your twelfth and final incarnation... and may I say you do not improve with age[135].

By the intermediate draft represented by the novelisation[136] this has become:

> 'The Valeyard, Doctor, is your penultimate reincarnation... Somewhere between your twelfth and thirteenth regeneration... and I may I say, you do not improve with age..!'[137]

The shooting script has:

> MASTER
>
> There is some evil in all of us, Doctor, even you. The

---

[135] While Robert Holmes had introduced the idea of a Time Lord being limited to 12 regenerations, (and thus 13 lives, as the first incarnation of a Time Lord has not yet regenerated) in his script for *The Deadly Assassin*, his draft conflates incarnations and regenerations in a way that suggests that either he was no longer au fait with how the terminology had come to be used in **Doctor Who** by the 1980s (e.g. in *The Five Doctors* (1983)) or that he had forgotten, or was uninterested in, his own work from a decade before. His confusion and conflation of details from 1960s and 1970s **Doctor Who** in his scripts for *The Two Doctors* suggests the latter explanation.

[136] See Chapter 2.

[137] Baker and Baker, *The Ultimate Foe* p26.

> Valeyard is an amalgamation of the dark side of your nature, somewhere between your twelfth and final incarnation... and I may say you do not improve with age.

What Anthony Ainley actually delivers onscreen is:

> 'There is some evil in all of us, Doctor, even you. The Valeyard is an amalgamation of the darker sides of your nature, somewhere between your twelfth and final incarnations... heh, and I may say you do not improve with age.'

Across these revisions, there is a process of muddying the nature of the Master's revelation so that the Valeyard's nature changes from the straightforward (he is a future, indeed the **final** incarnation of the Doctor) to the inchoate (he is an indeterminate figure between the penultimate and final Doctors, but also somehow the Doctor's penultimate incarnation) to the vaguely psychological (he is in some sense the Doctor's dark side, while also being from his own future, perhaps as a sort of warning).

It is not clear exactly when, or why, or by whom these changes were made. On his solo DVD commentary on Part 13, Saward is hazy about the details of the Valeyard's nature, and possibly unaware that the wording of the Master's revelation changed at least once after he left the **Doctor Who** production office for the last time.

Writing in DWM a decade later, John Nathan-Turner seemed to take at least some responsibility for this change, saying:

> 'I did not wish to "waste" a regenerative form on the Valeyard, so I'd always requested that the Valeyard be

considered the black side of the Doctor's character, somewhere between the last two regenerative forms[138]. That way future producers still had Doctors 12 and 13 at their disposal.' [139]

Taken with Saward's hazy recollection, Nathan-Turner's 'always' creates an indeterminacy over the exact timing of these changes, which the dates on the surviving draft scripts don't help to clear up.

These revisions though, represent a definite, gradual process of watering down the original intention for the story. This was, as Holmes' draft attests, simply that the Valeyard was a future incarnation of the Doctor, and that his motivation for his actions in the story would be to continue living by paradoxically stealing the lives of his earlier incarnation. Back in the summer of 1985 Saward had held a meeting with the writers he then intended to contribute to the 1986 series at the BBC's Threshold House. Holmes, David Halliwell and Jack Trevor Story were in attendance. Halliwell's notes from the meeting – dated Tuesday 9 July 1985, over a year before Parts 13 and 14 were recorded – record the intention that: 'Valeyard actually Dr in future regenerated form. Corrupt.'[140]

---

[138] This is an odd attitude to take when the episode under discussion features a character, the Master, who has successfully extended his own life beyond 13 incarnations, including in the first story in which the idea of a limited number of incarnations was introduced, and another, the Valeyard, who is attempting to do so. It was always surely obvious that **Doctor Who** would, in the event of the Doctor 'running out' of lives, simply introduce an in-story reason why he should not, as indeed happened in *The Time of the Doctor*.
[139] Nathan-Turner, 'This Must be the Place I Waited Years to Leave'.
[140] Molesworth, 'Bob's Fantasy Factory'.

It is also inarguably the case that Saward's version of Part 14 presents the character exactly as originally conceived. The Valeyard is written simply as a future incarnation of the Doctor. It is stated that if the Doctor is killed, the Valeyard, as a future incarnation of the same Time Lord, will cease to exist. In their final confrontation the Doctor ask the Valeyard 'How did I ever develop into such a pathetic individual?'

This is not the case in the Bakers' Part 14, which makes some attempt to square the circle of the transmitted version of Part 13's description of the Valeyard. The Master explains his desire to defeat the Valeyard by telling the Doctor that his morality gives the Master an advantage in their frequent battles, whereas the Valeyard ('A distillation of all that is evil in you, untainted by virtue, a composite of every dark thought...') is a different proposition. This builds on the Master's comment in Part 13 that he is 'not prepared to countenance a rival' (the Valeyard), but is very much more in keeping with the 'dark side' description of the Valeyard's character than the 'future, corrupt' one[141].

The Bakers have the Valeyard himself articulate his desire 'to be free' of the Doctor, whose very existence, never mind his 'constant crusading' he states 'restrains me'. He also chides himself for giving in to Doctorish 'urges' such as quoting from human literature. These lines together suggests a kind of Jungian Shadow self, who is not fully real or fully actualised while the Doctor himself exists. In the transmitted Part 14 Glitz refers to the Valeyard as the Doctor's

---

[141] The occasion in Part 13 where the Master says the Doctor and the Valeyard are 'one and the same person' is, tellingly, an untouched line of dialogue that has survived from Holmes' initial draft.

'other persona', which is not out of keeping with Jung and the idea of the Valeyard as the Doctor's shadow self. Some script-editing to Part 13 also helps shore up this interpretation. In all scripts for Part 13 the Doctor tells Glitz, 'I want you to meet my other self,' as they travel to see the Valeyard. Onscreen this has become 'I want you to meet my darker side'[142]. 'Other self' being the term used by the Doctor and others in both *The Three Doctors* (1972-73) and *The Five Doctors* (1983) to describe past and future incarnations of the same Time Lord, the amendment seems crucial and specific.

The Bakers make further detailed reference to this redrawing of the character in their novelisation. Chapter 11 has the Doctor thinking:

> 'Now he had to face the fact that the cold, calculating prosecutor was the personification of every deplorable act he had ever committed; every adverse deed he had ever contemplated. The malice he had learnt to govern had burst from its cage and been reincarnated into this monster known as the Valeyard.'[143]

Together these things make the Bakers' Valeyard's motivation for stealing the Doctor's lives a rather different matter to his simply being 'Just a pathetic old man' who has acted solely to 'extend your own miserable life', which is what the Doctor berates the Valeyard

---

[142] Intriguingly, a line cut from Holmes's draft has the Doctor refer to himself and the Valeyard as 'Id and Super-Id', a strange conflation of Jung and Freud that perhaps reflects feedback from the **Doctor Who** production office, tying in with Nathan-Turner's comment that he had 'always' wanted the Valeyard to be something more abstract than a later incarnation of the Doctor.

[143] Baker and Baker, *The Ultimate Foe* p64.

for being at the conclusion of Saward's version of Part 14[144].

In many ways, the distinctions make the Valeyard a significantly different character in terms of motivation, action and execution. It is to Michael Jayston's infinite credit that his performance in the two episodes that were shot smooths over such radically different conceptions of the part he has been asked to play. (It would perhaps have been better for all concerned had the 'future' aspect of the Valeyard's origin been disposed of during script editing, making him unambiguously a kind of Mr Hyde to the Doctor's Dr Jekyll[145], an id to the Doctor's superego.)

The Valeyard is mentioned only once in televised **Doctor Who** after *The Trial of a Time Lord*, by the Great Intelligence (Richard E Grant) to the Doctor's friends Madame Vastra, Jenny and Strax on Trenzalore during *The Name of the Doctor* (2013), and then only as a continuity grace note. There the Intelligence lists 'the Valeyard' as 'a name he [the Doctor] will have before the end' (i.e. his death). This seems more in keeping with the original conception of the character than the Bakers' shadow-self version. Yet by the end of 2013's **Doctor Who** episodes we have learned that the Doctor as played by Matt Smith is in actuality the Time Lord's 13th

---

[144] Sadly, the intriguing idea that whatever the Valeyard's level of corruption it is, on some level, less immoral to steal these lives from himself than from some other Time Lord, is never touched upon by any draft of any episode of this serial.

[145] *Strange Case of Dr Jekyll and Mr Hyde* was first published in 1886. The 1887 theatrical adaptation was playing in London during the Whitechapel murders. The actor playing both parts, Richard Mansfield (1857-1907) was suspected by the public, although not the police, of being the killer, and he and his production have become a standard part of Ripper conspiracy theorising.

incarnation, and seen him escape the death that the Intelligence was referring to in the past tense and regenerate into a new form[146]. This leaves no room for a 'future' Doctor to be the Valeyard, unless he is a later incarnation than Smith's – and as of the time of writing two further Doctors, Peter Capaldi and Jodie Whittaker, have been cast who are evidently not the Valeyard either[147]. It also means that a Doctor 'between your twelfth and final incarnation' (as the Master says onscreen) would appear at any point after David Tennant's Doctor.[148]

That a single line of dialogue about the character can prompt the paragraph above is an indication of how convoluted and contradictory the very idea of the Valeyard had become by the

---

[146] *The Time of the Doctor.*

[147] The events of *The Time of the Doctor* explicitly rewrite the Doctor's future, despite his death on Trenzalore being established as a past event in *The Name of the Doctor*. Logically, the future described in *The Trial of a Time Lord* is one that predates the changes to his timeline wrought by the 2013 story.

[148] Fans have speculated that this is indeed the case, and the one-hearted half-human duplicate of the David Tennant Doctor created during *Journey's End* (2008) will go on to become the Valeyard. Nothing on screen rules this out, but it is both tonally at odds with *Journey's End* itself, and frankly a **terrible** idea that anyone should be embarrassed for advocating. In fact the concept that emerges in *The Trial of a Time Lord* is oddly like that of Cho-Je in *Planet of the Spiders* (1974), a 'projection' of a future self, between regenerations, perhaps one which the Doctor avoided becoming. While it is unlikely the Bakers, or even Nathan-Turner, were aware of the details of this serial, Holmes had been assistant script editor on it, and became the series Script Editor with *Robot* (1974-75), the next story in production, so would have had access to and read the scripts, even if he did not remember them by 1986.

time *The Trial of a Time Lord* was transmitted. As Philip Martin noted shortly after transmission, 'when we reached the final episode I couldn't follow it! And I had been there at the beginning!'[149]

This is a shame, as the original conception is clear, simple and strong. So much so it is summed up in a single, sadly later revised, line of dialogue from one of the Doctor's old enemies. Let's return to that clarity in preparation for looking, in our next chapter, at a draft that that conception underlies.

MASTER

The Valeyard, Doctor, is your twelfth and final incarnation... and may I say you do not improve with age.

---

[149] Cornell, Paul, 'Philip Martin Interview', DWM #125.

CHAPTER 4: PART 14 BY ERIC SAWARD

When he withdrew his script, although pre-production was at an advanced stage, Saward had as yet not signed a contract to deliver the episode as a freelance writer, probably because when he began it he was still on the BBC staff[150]. As such, it was a simple matter for him, legally, to refuse permission for the BBC to produce a script they had, strictly speaking, not yet bought the right to produce[151].

What was far from simple was the situation now facing Nathan-Turner. The draft scripts had been sent to the cast, and the episode was already in rehearsal. All copies would have to be recalled and shredded, and a new Part 14 written from scratch.

While the immediate consequence of this decision were chiefly faced by Nathan-Turner and 7C's director, Chris Clough, Saward's actions should not be seen as a fit of consequence-free pique on his part. Withdrawing the script meant the newly freelance writer surrendered his fees for writing the episode, for any future foreign

---

[150] Practices such as this are not unusual in the history of **Doctor Who**. To pick an example almost entirely at random, then Story Editor Gerry Davis' scripts for *The Highlanders* (1966-67) were retrospectively commissioned on 12 December 1966, after two of them had already been shot. Due to another writer's failure to deliver, Davis needed to put the scripts together so quickly that the formal niceties of commissioning were postponed until after the immediate crisis had passed.

[151] He also attempted to withdraw permission to use his version of Part 13, meaning the production office would have had to revert to using Holmes' first draft, which Saward himself had considered unsuitable, but it was ruled that Saward had undertaken his revisions to the earlier episode in his capacity as Script Editor, while a contracted BBC staff member.

sales and repeats, and for any subsequent commercial home releases. Saward was effectively turning down the novelisation of Parts 13 and 14 at the same time[152]. While Saward did not have to deal with the production fallout of his decision, he was sacrificing both immediate and future income by withdrawing from the production.

Like Holmes' Part 13, Saward's Part 14 also survives, although in this case there are multiple copies of it in existence[153]. Like Holmes' Part 13, it is divided into 'Telecines' (scenes assumed to be shot on location) and 'Scenes' (assumed to be recorded in a BBC studio)

---

[152] WH Allen's policy at the time was to give any living **Doctor Who** scriptwriter first refusal on writing the novelisation of their own scripts. This applied even to veterans of the 1960s series, some of whom had almost forgotten they had ever written for the series, and were surprised to be contacted as part of WH Allen's by then systematic programme of attempting to create a complete library of **Doctor Who** in print. While the long-term financial rewards of writing an episode of **Doctor Who** can be exaggerated, it is worth noting that *The Trial of a Time Lord* has been available commercially continuously since late 1993, and indeed the novelisation *The Ultimate Foe* is in print in audiobook form at time of writing, available both on disc and as a digital download. While he ceased any involvement in television **Doctor Who** in 1986, Saward did write the novelisation of *Attack of the Cybermen* in 1989, and would later contribute to BBC video, audio and DVD releases of and related to the series.

[153] Having been issued to so many people it would be surprising if it did not. A copy of the 1968 **Doctor Who** script 'The Prison in Space', abandoned at a similar stage of pre-production, would be uncovered in his home by then-regular cast member Frazer Hines in the 21st century.

which are numbered separately. There are nine Telecines and 23 studio scenes.

Beginning the story, Telecines 1 to 4 and Scenes 1 to 4 form a seven page sequence in which a character on location and another in the studio argue with one another, with most cuts constituting a 'scene break' even though the action is continuous.

Telecine 1 begins with the Doctor on the beach, drowning in sand. As he does so he insists to the Valeyard that his death will not result in the Valeyard inheriting his remaining lives. The Valeyard, still in voiceover as at the end of Part 13, replies that the Doctor has already signed them away. The Doctor objects that he signed his lives to Mr JJ Chambers, and the Valeyard retorts that 'for the sake of this charade I am JJ Chambers'.

Scene 1 is set in 'The Valeyard's Control Room', where the argument continues. This set is described as:

> '(Possibly re-dressed bridge of ship)

> 'Anyway, hi-tech with a large screen on which we can see the Doctor. Somewhere in the room is a sealed entrance to what we shall later learn is a Time Vent.'

As with Popplewick's office in Part 13, Saward is assuming that sets constructed for Parts 9 to 12 will be available, and that it will be an effective cost-saving measure to reuse them for any non-location, non-Courtroom scenes. The Valeyard does not have a 'Control Room' in the broadcast Part 14, but there are several scenes set in the Master's TARDIS' console room, the set for which is simply that for the Doctor's TARDIS painted black[154]. It is a fair assumption, then, that these scenes would have been staged on that set instead, had the episode reached production. This makes sense, given that the Valeyard is the Doctor[155]. The set, after all, was in storage, features a large scanner screen and had a section with a door that could be simply redressed to become the sealed entrance to the Time Vent.

In Scene 1 the Valeyard taunts the Doctor, by saying that he has perfected 'the talent for mind control and illusion which you chose, in your misguided youth, to neglect,' leading the Doctor to respond that illusion is 'for the theatre, not real life'. Cutting to the Mud Flats and Telecine 2, the Doctor continues, provoking the Valeyard by claiming illusion is 'only seriously practiced nowadays by the children's entertainers and the weak minded'. The Valeyard accuses the Doctor of provocation, and the Doctor responds by pointing out that the High Council may no longer be in any position to ratify the Valeyard's contract.

Back in the Valeyard's control room for Scene 2, the Valeyard insists his contract is 'inviolable'. The Doctor insists that if the Valeyard truly believed that, he would have killed him 'at the first opportunity', and the Valeyard responds by saying that he wishes to enjoy the sensation of paradoxically surviving his own suicide. Back on the Mud Flats for Scene 3, the argument continues, with Doctor asserting that the Valeyard has lost his nerve, and knows that '[t]oo many games have been played with the [M]atrix' for the Valeyard to be sure that killing the Doctor will not result in his own

---

[154] Because he's evil.
[155] And evil.

death as a future incarnation of the same Time Lord. He then points out that the Valeyard would be the chief prosecution witness in any trial of the High Council over Ravolox. His fellow conspirators will want him dead to ensure his silence.

Scene 3 is again in the Valeyard's control room. The scanner screen fills with static (described in the script as 'shush') and Glitz, who has been standing silently by the Valeyard since Scene 1, is enraged that the Valeyard has killed the Doctor. The Valeyard insists that his earlier incarnation is unharmed, and that the screen is now unclear because '[a]nother mind is attempting to break into my illusion.'

Telecine 4 returns us to the mud flats for a final time. The Master arrives and rescues the Doctor from the mud, the two exchange insults, and then the Doctor apologises and thanks the Master. The two then concentrate, turning the mud flats around them back into the streets around the Fantasy Factory by force of will. The Master explains that the Valeyard is using the power of the Matrix to sustain his world of illusion, and that consequently the Master himself is having to use 'massive amounts of energy' to sustain his own presence in the Matrix[156]. Having explained this, he disappears, leaving the Doctor to walk gingerly around the barrel that attacked him in Part 13, before engaging in another argument with the Valeyard's disembodied voice.

Scene 4 again briefly returns us to the Valeyard's control room, where Glitz taunts the Valeyard, saying that the Doctor is right, and

---

[156] The need for this power, assuming he has physically entered the Matrix through the Seventh Door as the Doctor and Glitz did, is never explained (and indeed he exits the Matrix using that door in Scene 22).

that the Valeyard is afraid the High Council has 'got at' his contract. This is followed by Telecine 5, an establishing model shot of the space station, and Scene 5, which is set in the courtroom and features the Inquisitor, the Keeper of the Matrix and Melanie. The Keeper says he finds the Master confusing, but fears that whatever he does will be for selfish reasons, and Melanie responds that the Doctor feels that way about most Time Lords. News is brought that, thanks to the Master's revelations about Ravolox, the entire High Council has resigned. The Inquisitor fears that, should the news that 'the [M]atrix has been violated' also leak, Gallifrey would collapse into civil war.

Scene 6 takes us back to the Valeyard's control room again. The Valeyard says that the Doctor's thoughts are confusing and wonders why he should be thinking about 'a plant?' – a 'mel-bush'[157]. Glitz informs him that the Doctor's companion's name is Mel[158]. The Valeyard then decides to use Mel to trap the Doctor 'in a very safe place'.

Telecine 6 is another alleyway scene. The Doctor is approached by a Monk with gnarled monstrous hands. The Monk throws back his hood, revealing himself to be Mr Popplewick, wearing gloves to suggest he's a monster. The Doctor asks if Popplewick has a 'fetish'

---

[157] Melanie's surname, 'Bush', was included in the **Doctor Who** production office's writers' guide to the character issued on 5 July 1985, but was ultimately never used onscreen.

[158] The Valeyard should know this, not simply because he is a future Doctor, but given the events of Parts 9 to 12. But then Saward had not read Parts 10 to 12. Glitz's seemingly lecherous description of Melanie as 'a bit of siddle' might be seen to bizarrely foreshadow their decision to travel together after she leaves the Doctor in *Dragonfire* (1987) episode 3.

for 'dressing up' or whether he is paid to do so, and when Popplewick mocks his hostility threatens to 'flatten' him. Popplewick complains that he is just a messenger, and the Doctor points out that the ancient Greeks killed messengers who brought bad news. Popplewick says he brings good news. Mr Chambers has granted the Doctor an appointment. The Doctor agrees to follow him, and Popplewick says that they have to collect Melanie first: she has followed the Doctor into the Matrix.

Scene 7 is set in the Valeyard's control room, where the Valeyard explains to Glitz that he will demonstrate to him 'the power of the most perfect geometrical shape', leading into Scene 8[159]. In this Popplewick leads the Doctor into a tunnel, where both meet Melanie. Popplewick disappears, and the Doctor and Mel find themselves unable to escape the circular tunnel, which seemingly has no entries or exits. Realising they are going round in circles, their conversation becomes 'obsessed by circumambulation'. Added to which a degree of circumloquacious circumvolution has edged into our vocabulary.'[160] The Doctor realises that Melanie is unreal and that he is trapped in a circle inside his own mind. Popplewick reappears, saying it was thought this trap would 'confuse you good

---

[159] Although 'Scene 8' had de facto been intended to be recorded in the studio, Chris Clough had found a pottery kiln at the Gladstone Pottery Museum which Saward later described as the 'perfect location' for this scene (indeed so perfect he, decades later, expressed regret it had never been recorded there). Had this script reached production, Scene 8 would logistically have had to be renumbered as a Telecine or redesignated 'OB' (as happened with some Popplewicks material in Part 13) to indicate this. We'll continue to use the designations of the draft we have.

[160] This again seems to invoke Dickens' Circumlocution Office.

and proper' before showing the Doctor back out to the Alleyway for Telecine 7 and once again vanishing into thin air, this time leaving his robes behind when he does so.

Scene 9 begins with Glitz dismissing Scene 8 and Telecine 7 to the Valeyard as a 'a bit of a waste of time'. When the Valeyard demands to know why Glitz, like all fools, keeps stating the obvious, Glitz points out that by doing so people like him are able to get supposedly cleverer 'super brains' to admit things they don't otherwise want to say. Glitz demands to know what the Valeyard will do if it turns out the Doctor is right and his contract with the High Council won't be honoured. The Valeyard replies that, if he is to die, '[t]hen everything dies.' Glitz protests, and says he understands that it's disappointing 'when a caper falls apart' but that even criminals have to have rules. The Valeyard can't commit genocide and still expect to be taken seriously as an honest crook: 'The public won't put up with it!' The Valeyard maintains that he is serious.

Scene 10 features the Master returning to the Trial Room's screen. The Inquisitor and the Keeper are discussing how the Valeyard's contract with the High Council has been revoked. The Master informs them that if the Valeyard discovers this, he will kill everyone and everything, and that he has the power to do so. The Master has discovered that the Valeyard's base is over a Time Vent. The Keeper explains to the court that 'If the Valeyard does open the vent, an irratic [sic[161]] surge of time will enter our stabilized

---

[161] It is unclear if this spelling is an error or a coinage of new jargon. If the latter, it could be taken to be meant to imply that the surge of time will 'irritate' normal time, due to it having caustic properties. Thus I have retained it here.

continuum. The effect will be devastating – like mixing matter and anti-matter'. Mel pleads that the Valeyard must be stopped, while the Keeper calculates that the vent can be open for a maximum of 72 seconds before reality 'would be irrevocably damaged'. The Inquisitor decides that the Valeyard's contract should be reinstated to the Matrix, meaning he would have no reason to use the Time Vent. The Master points out that doing so would cost the Doctor his life, and the Keeper agrees that giving the Valeyard the Doctor's future incarnations would also create an unacceptable precedent. The Inquisitor points out that if time is destroyed by the Valeyard, precedent as a concept will cease to have any meaning.

Scene 11 features the Valeyard, still in his control room, realising that the contract has been revoked following the fall of the High Council, and priming the explosive bolts of on the door to the Time Vent in response.

Telecine 7 take us back to the Fantasy Factory exterior. The Doctor is trying to pick the lock of its door. He realises that someone behind him is holding an object to his head. Something that both he and the audience, according to stage directions, think is the barrel of a gun. The Doctor looks up and he and realising that it's the Master, who is making a 'gun' with his fingers. The Master explains that the High Council wanted the Doctor dead. The Doctor asks why the Master doesn't oblige them, becoming a hero in the process. The Master rejects the idea, saying 'And spoil my anti-establishment image – I don't think so.' The Master then informs the Doctor that the High Council's contract with the Valeyard has indeed been removed from the Matrix, meaning that if he – or anyone else – kills the Doctor, the Valeyard will sense it, before then dying himself[162]. However, he will have enough time to open the Time Vent and take the rest of reality with him when he goes. The Master points out that now only the Doctor can get physically close enough to the Valeyard to stop him, and wishes him luck. The Master disappears, and the Doctor calls out for the Valeyard.

Scene 12, back in the Valeyard's control room, sees the Doctor appear on the Valeyard's scanner screen, and offer to make a deal with the Valeyard. The conversation continues in Telecine 9, where the Doctor explains that the Master has told him about the Time Vent, and that as a consequence he agrees to surrender his remaining incarnations to the Valeyard. Scene 13 features the Valeyard briefly doubting the Doctor's trustworthiness, and Telecine 10 continues their dialogue further, as the Doctor insists that the High Council's agreement is irrelevant and the two of them can make their own deal instead. In response to this the Valeyard lets the Doctor into his control room.

Scene 14 shows the Master reporting back to the Court that the Doctor is now with the Valeyard, and then allowing the court's inhabitants to see what is transpiring there, leading to Scene 15.

In this the Doctor is saddened to discover that his future self has already primed the bolts on the Time Vent door. The Valeyard asks if the Doctor thought he was bluffing, to which the Doctor responds that he hoped that he was. The Doctor calls the Valeyard 'just a

---

[162] This is the same logic expressed by the Colin Baker Doctor when he fears history has changed and the Patrick Troughton Doctor has died in the second episode of Holmes's *The Two Doctors*. This may mean it reflects some of Holmes's intentions for Part 14. It may alternatively be Saward riffing on the work of a writer he admired.

pathetic old man' and the Valeyard realises that the Doctor's offer of a private deal was itself a bluff. The Doctor denounces his future self as 'a pathetic individual' who has connived in the destruction of their favourite planet, destroyed the credibility of the Matrix and shredded the last of the Time Lords' reputation, purely so he can 'extend [his] miserable life'. Provoked, the Valeyard opens the Time Vent.

Scene 16, in the Trial Room, has the Inquisitor wonder why the Doctor has done this, and in Scene 17 both she and the audience find out. The Doctor grabs the Valeyard and the two of them together tumble into the Time Vent. In Scene 18, the court reacts to this with shock, with the Keeper noting that the Doctor has done this deliberately. Scene 19 shows us the inside of the Time Vent, with the Doctor and the Valeyard struggling as they 'freefall down the spiralling vent'. Back in the Valeyard's control room for Scene 20, the Master appears on the screen and commands Glitz to close and secure the Time Vent, and then leave the Matrix, as the Valeyard's illusion is breaking up now he is no longer there to sustain it. In Scene 21, the Keeper in the Trial Room confirms that Glitz closed the Time Vent before the damage to reality became irreparable, and in Scene 22 the Master and Glitz stagger out of the Matrix and into the corridor outside the Trial Room. An exhausted Glitz says he will retire, but the Master points out that with 'the Doctor out of the way' he now has free rein: 'The universe is ours.' Climbing back into the casket in which he arrived, Glitz tells the Master, 'I'll tell you what [...] you can have my half as well', an offer which, with some amusement, the Master accepts.

Back in the Trial Room for Scene 23, Melanie asks to be returned to her own time and planet, which the Inquisitor promises to have done. Mel says that she will miss the Doctor, and asks if his body will ever be found. The Keeper says that he cannot risk opening the Time Vent, and if the Doctor or the Valeyard gets out, it will have to be by their own efforts. Mel is amazed, she thought the Doctor was dead. The script ends with Scene 24, the Doctor and Valeyard 'falling and tumbling' through the Vent, while in voice-over the Inquisitor explains that the Valeyard and the Doctor are both alive, but trapped. '[G]etting out of that mess won't be easy,' says the Keeper's voice. 'I'm sure the Doctor'll succeed – he must!' says Mel. 'If he doesn't,' replies the Keeper, 'the vent will remain [h]is prison for all eternity!'

Nathan-Turner and Saward's dispute over this script principally concerned this ending, which Nathan-Turner did not like. The Producer saw the cliffhanger as making the series end with 'an enormous question-mark over the future of the show.'[163] He requested that it be changed. Saward saw this as Nathan-Turner 'reneging' on their agreement to follow Holmes' story. Saward wrote to Nathan-Turner, saying:

> 'This type of ending had been planned from the very beginning. I am also certain that I told you, albeit a long time ago, what was proposed. Even if I hadn't, I will continue to argue in favour of this type of end of season conclusion. I think it's stronger, more gripping and gives you the opportunity to take [**Doctor Who**] wherever you want next season – for it certainly needs to go further than it did this

---

[163] Nathan-Turner, 'This Must be the Place I Waited Years to Leave'. Ironically, Saward had criticised Nathan-Turner's passion for inserting a literal question-mark motif into the Doctor's clothing.

one! (as I was responsible for 10 of its episodes, I mean that kindly).'[164]

While Saward's climax is dramatic, It is hard to see much value in his assertion that the complex situation the Doctor is left in at the end of his script is a good jumping-off point for any future revamp of **Doctor Who**. Logically, Nathan-Turner's preferred ending, the Doctor being acquitted and leaving with Melanie in the TARDIS, means the next series can begin with it landing anywhere and in virtually any kind of story[165]. By contrast, the conclusion of Saward's Part 14 would require at least some explanation in whatever was made next, tying the next story into the Trial story, inherently preventing any sort of clean break[166]. Nevertheless, both men felt very strongly about their respective positions. Saward wrote to the Producer, making clear that he would not change the ending at any price:

> 'I feel in my very bones that your 'walkdown' ending is wrong. It's weak, far too predictable and, anyway, we've seen it all before. Neither is it very dramatic. If you don't like my ending – fine. If you want to suggest an alternative strong, powerful and **dramatic** ending, I will, subject to discussion, happily incorporate it, but not your current suggestion.'[167]

---

[164] BBC WAC T65/224, letter from Saward to Nathan-Turner, 26 May 1986.

[165] And indeed with any occupants if, as transpired in reality, there were cast changes after the episode's recording.

[166] Unless the cliffhanger were simply ignored, which can hardly have been Saward's intention.

[167] BBC WAC T65/224, letter dated 26 May 1986.

That much of *The Trial of a Time Lord*'s structure is derived from Dickens's *A Christmas Carol* is often noted[168]. The Doctor's adventures on Ravolox represents the (recent) past, and those on Thoros Beta the present[169]. What is less often considered is that, at least in the original conception, the Valeyard, rather than the adventure on *Hyperion III*, is the Doctor's future and absolutely literally so.

Also relevant, and ignored, in discussion of 1986's **Doctor Who**, is how Dickens's story ends. Having seen a future in which he dies unloved and alone, Ebenezer Scrooge mends his ways and, by the narrator's account, aborts the future he has seen through this action ('Tiny Tim [...] did NOT die,'[170]). It is not at all difficult to see how the logic of this ending underpins Saward's Part 14. The Doctor is faced with a future incarnation of himself, who is not only corrupt, but selfish to the point where he is prepared to kill literally everyone else alive if he himself cannot go on living. Horrified by this, the Doctor demonstrates that he is not yet the Valeyard, by willingly dying to stop his future self's act of mass murder[171]. This is

---

[168] And Halliwell's notes indicate this was always a deliberate choice (Molesworth, 'Bob's Fantasy Factory').

[169] The Doctor is, after all, 'taken out of time' to be tried: his present is running along a corridor on Thoros Beta, his presence in the courtroom an interruption. This conceit would be better expressed if he were returned there in any version of the story's conclusion.

[170] Dickens, Charles, *A Christmas Carol* p116.

[171] The 2017 **Doctor Who** story *World Enough And Time / The Doctor Falls* presents a story in in which the Master (John Simm) murders his future incarnation Missy (Michelle Gomez) because he will not tolerate a future self who will, reformed, choose to stand alongside the Doctor simply because it is the right thing to do. The

something that, by the logic the episode itself articulates, would cancel out the Valeyard's own existence, in the same way Scrooge's newfound selflessness erased the future in which Tiny Tim died of his infirmities within a year.

'Our' Doctor sacrificing himself to stop a 'future' Doctor who is only concerned with his own survival is an effective statement about the Doctor as a character, **especially** when applied to the Doctor as characterised over the two then most recent series. Saward has described a decision to make the Doctor of *The Twin Dilemma* (1984) more 'energetic' in the aftermath of his regeneration than the 'passive' newly regenerated Doctor of *Castrovalva* (1982). This intention resulted in a scene in which, deranged by the process, he physically assaults Peri, seemingly with the intention of choking her to death with his bare hands. Subsequent episodes saw the new Doctor's initial characterisation marked by bursts of bad temper and sudden violence that seemed, if not out of character, then dissonant. The character is also often written as slightly distant from the people around him, but in a way that often comes across as uncaring, even dissociative, rather than 'alien'[172]. (Something

---

character movement is the same, while being a moral inversion.

[172] It is the material, rather than the performance, that is at fault, and it is noticeable that Colin Baker's very best work in the role on television is in scripts by the Bakers and Robert Holmes. Holmes, along with many **Doctor Who** writers, considered the differences between onscreen incarnations of the Doctor to be simply a matter of the actors' interpretations, always writing the same character regardless of who was in the part. Holmes' Doctor is, across his work on **Doctor Who**, noticeably more bad-tempered than many other writers', but *The Two Doctors* episode 2 and *The Trial of a Time Lord* Part 1 give Baker opportunities to be wistful and even elegiac, which he seizes. Pip and Jane Baker's Doctor is a jollier,

that continues in this draft of Part 14, where the Doctor threatens to 'flatten' Mr Popplewick when he becomes bored with their conversation.)

A future Doctor who has become so uncaring he presents as a genocidal villain, effectively shocking 'our' Doctor off a path he has unknowingly embarked on since his regeneration, is a strong idea. It serves both as a course correction for issues in the writing of the series in the mid-1980s, and as an effective way of building some of those missteps into a character arc of exactly the kind Baker had, as an actor, wanted to play, having always expressed a desire for his Doctor to go on a 'journey' as a character. In comparison, Tom Baker regarded the Doctor's character as essentially immobile and undevelopable[173].

There is an argument that elements of this shift in characterisation[174], with which Saward is closely associated, began earlier, when the Doctor was still played by Peter Davison, and only became overt after the opportunities presented by the Doctor being recast.

Episode 3 of Saward's first script, *The Visitation*, has the Doctor's

---

warmer figure than Saward's. He is still given to sarcasm and bad temper, but is more sober, affectionate and less easily provoked. Colin Baker has expressed admiration for the Bakers' characterisation of his Doctor and concurs with prevailing opinion that Holmes was 'the greatest' of 20th-century **Doctor Who** writers.

[173] **The Lively Arts**: *Whose Doctor Who* (1977); Freeman, John, 'Talking to Tom Baker', DWM #180.

[174] Which may or may not be seen as distinct from 'character development'.

sonic screwdriver destroyed (at Nathan-Turner's request) and in the next episode the he picks up a gun and uses it to shoot out a lock instead, proudly saying 'I never miss'. While the only thing damaged is a door – and guest character Richard Mace's pride – this moment seems to prefigure the strange truth that all subsequent stories written by Saward see the Doctor not only using but firing and even killing with guns. It is not an exaggeration to say that the Doctor uses firearms more often in the stories Saward wrote, let alone edited[175], than the rest of the series prior put together.

This already is worth remarking on but is yet more interesting when paired with other developments in the series at this time. It is another feature of the stories Saward wrote that the Doctor is peripheral to the resolution of the drama, events being resolved by historical circumstance (*The Visitation, Earthshock, Slipback* (Radio 4, 1985)) or by other characters committing violent – often suicidally violent – acts the Doctor is not prepared to, in order to frustrate the serial's antagonist's plans (*Resurrection of the Daleks, Revelation of the Daleks*).

If we expand our remit to stories that Saward commissioned from other writers and developed all the way to screen, it becomes very

---

[175] The Doctor uses firearms so often in the 1985 series that when he refuses a gun in *The Mark of the Rani* this is drawn attention to, and he says 'Oh, no thanks. I've given them up. Guns can seriously damage your health, you know.' (*The Mark of the Rani* episode 2). The exchange is not present in the Bakers' novelisation of the serial which is, in keeping with their practice, based on their own final drafts scripts rather than the transmitted programme, suggesting Saward was its author.

apparent how often the Doctor contributes little to how matters conclude (e.g. *Mawdryn Undead* (1983) is resolved by a coincidence, *Enlightenment* (1983) by Turlough's choice) and that when he does, it is through violence, including the use of guns (e.g. *Arc of Infinity* (1983)) or even chemical warfare (*Warriors of the Deep* (1984)). The last example is key. While it is clear that the Doctor's actions on Seabase 4 represent a failure to live up to his own ideals, his final line 'There should have been another way' could be taken to mean that there was not, and that the Doctor was right to resort to a gas attack[176].

The following story, *The Awakening* (1984), sees the villain, Sir George Hutchinson, killed by another guest character, Will Chandler, who opines 'It be better he be dead' by way of justification[177]. Again, the implication is that murder is the only way to resolve the situation. Saward's own *Resurrection of the Daleks*[178] sees the Doctor shoot a Dalek mutant with a 20th-century handgun in episode 1[179], and commit another gas attack in order to clear the

---

[176] *Warriors of the Deep* episode 4.

[177] *The Awakening* episode 2. By his own account, this story's scripts (credited to Eric Pringle) were entirely written by Saward (Russell, Gary, 'Writing Doctor Who: Eric Saward', DWM #148).

[178] Between these two stories is *Frontios*, in which the Doctor wins by trickery and then spares his enemy. It is possibly relevant that its author was Christopher H Bidmead, whose earliest work on **Doctor Who** predated Saward's.

[179] The second time he fires a recognisable modern weapon in the programme. The first, in *Image of the Fendahl* (1977), sees him fire a shotgun loaded with rock salt, rather than shot. In *The Seeds of Doom* (1976) he briefly waves a stolen gun while escaping, but this explicitly a bluff: 'You'd never use it!' says Sarah Jane, 'True. But they don't know that, do they?' he replies (episode 4). There are

area of Daleks in episode 2. More importantly, episode 2 also sees the Doctor decide to execute Davros, but he is unable to pull the trigger after Davros taunts him about his weakness. This is the second occasion in two successive Saward-scripted stories – after *Earthshock* – where the Doctor argues about ethics with one of his returning monsters and **loses**[180]. The story is then resolved by a guest character committing a suicide bombing to save the day.

Taken together, these examples seem to indicate a programme arguing that its own lead character's established approach to the situations in which he finds himself is insufficient. That, as Davros argues (and unlike Will Chandler or Stein) the Doctor 'lacks the courage' to commit violent acts when necessary[181]. In this context, the new Doctor's willingness to pick up guns[182] takes on a new light. It also makes the newly regenerated Doctor's killing of Mestor in *The Twin Dilemma* episode 4 seem like a statement of intent, and the Doctor's later actions a deliberate follow on from it. (Although, despite his increased propensity for violence, the Doctor remains peripheral to many stories in the 1985 series, most notably

---

other examples of the Doctor briefly handling period weaponry, e.g. *The Gunfighters* (1966) sees him repeatedly trying to give one away as a running joke, while he uses an antique hunting rifle on a giant rat in *The Talons of Weng-Chiang*, set c1890.

[180] In *Earthshock* it was a Cyberleader whom the Doctor later defeated by shooting him repeatedly in the chest with his own gun.

[181] *Resurrection of the Daleks* episode 2.

[182] Saward's novelisation of *Attack of the Cybermen* features details concerning guns unusual in **Doctor Who** (e.g. make and model numbers on pp26, 65). A scene in which the Doctor and (the American) Peri discuss the United Kingdom's ostensibly restrictive attitude to private ownership of firearms was deleted from the script for episode 1 of the same story at a late stage.

Saward's *Revelation of the Daleks*).

Saward's Part 14 gives the Doctor the suicidally violent role previously taken by guest characters, placing him at the centre of the resolution of the drama, in both plot and character terms, and it seems to do so with reference to the character's recent greater propensity for violence and marginalisation within his own series. It may be this thematic movement, rather than the physical situation, that Saward saw as giving future **Doctor Who** a springboard to go anywhere it liked, in which case he has a point. The Doctor could emerge from his confrontation with the Valeyard either renewed and reinvigorated as to his mission, who he is and what he needs to do in order to win, or as a more sombre figure, alive to his potential for evil and thus more cautious of indulging his darker impulses, depending on what Baker wanted to play and what Nathan-Turner wanted the series to be like in the immediate future.

None of this, ultimately, was to be.

> 'John, untypically, because he never told me what was going on behind the scenes, told me that there were issues. Eric had written a story which in John's eyes killed off **Doctor Who**, and gave the BBC the option of finishing the programme there and then. [He] asked Eric not to do that, Eric refused and wouldn't change the script, so Eric walked out, John was left with a last episode he couldn't use.'
>
> [Colin Baker]
>
> 'I thought it was the perfect out for the season – what better can you get than your hero trapped for eternity in this place? I didn't want to soften it and have them live happily every after, which I really thought would undercut it

and it was one of the reasons I said "Let's forget this, it isn't working. Your ideas and my ideas are too at variance.'"

[Eric Saward]

Thematically and dramatically, Saward's ending is the ending of the story *The Trial of a Time Lord* tells. As Saward observes on his commentary on the DVD of the transmitted version of Part 13, it features 'all this other stuff that's leading to this moment,' that then never arrives. By far the strongest aspect of Saward's draft is that ending, and were it to be removed or amended, the script would lose much, if not all, of the appeal and drama that, as written, it has. It would also stop the story making any sort of thematic sense. The script has many other issues, but it is not to Nathan-Turner's credit that what he fixated on as the episode's main flaw was in fact its strongest aspect.

What else is there to be said about Saward's script? It's a thin episode, not merely in the number of pages but also in terms of what happens on them. The Valeyard's contract with the Time Lords is withdrawn from the Matrix, and then restored. The Doctor and the Valeyard argue about its validity every time they speak. The Master flits between the courtroom, where he elucidates the plot to the Inquisitor in a strange reversal of the trial format of Parts 1 to 12, and the Matrix, seemingly without particular purpose. He has stated his motivation in Part 13, but it is not returned to or elaborated upon[183], and this reflects another key issue with the script, it's not entirely clear why a lot of the characters are doing what they're doing, except because circumstances have forced them to be where they are.

---

[183] Something the Bakers' Part 14 does do: see Chapter 5.

Melanie merely stays in the courtroom and reacts. So does the Inquisitor. So does the Keeper of the Matrix, while still having a larger role than in the transmitted Part 14. Here he at least gets to calculate the danger of the Time Vent using his professional expertise, and is given the serial's final line. (Actor James Bree was disappointed with the replacement Part 14, in which his part was smaller and consequently less fun to play[184].)

Glitz too is restricted to a single set (the Valeyard's 'control room'), except for a few seconds in the anteroom outside the court right at the episode's conclusion. While Glitz is the kind of character that Saward's writing usually finds attractive, and he provides an effective foil for the Doctor in Part 13, here he is underused to the point of seeming neglected.

This is also true, most surprisingly, of Mr Popplewick. Popplewick is Saward's own creation, and in Part 13 a hugely entertaining character, both on the page and onscreen, yet here the character appears briefly, and then without reference to the obsession with procedure and order that defines him in Part 13. He is also no longer a clerk. He is now, in a move that seems to be arch for its own sake, a monk. It may be that, despite Popplewick's characterisation being Saward's, his **function**, which is directly copied from Bencray's in Holmes' draft, defeated Saward, leaving

---

[184] Marson, 'Pip and Jane Baker'; Hearn, 'Writing Who'. An intention for the Keeper's role to be larger does make sense. Bree was a well-regarded character actor whose earlier roles in **Doctor Who** (*The War Games* and *Full Circle* (1980)), as well as television generally, are substantial guest-star roles. More inexpensive actors could easily fulfilled the part of the Keeper as transmitted. (See also footnote 65.)

him with a character without a purpose, reduced to playing a weak practical joke on the Doctor (and the audience) and the subject of a bizarre barbed response from the Doctor who makes insinuations about his sexuality and threatens to beat him up. This could simply be a result of the problem that the Part 13 rewrite was intended to eliminate, of his not knowing the details of Holmes' planned conclusion.

These characters' roles are not reduced to buy the series' ostensible lead more to do, even though there are two versions of him in this story, a story which is about him fighting himself. This script's Valeyard is both strikingly different from, and far less prominent than, the version in the transmitted episode. While the character presented here is more conceptually interesting than that which eventually reached the screen (see 'Intermission: Who Is the Valeyard'), the Valeyard too is restricted to a single set, punching buttons and scowling, before being taken out by the Doctor in a physical struggle. While this fits with the characterisation of him as a 'pathetic old man', it is almost a shock reading this draft now, in the context of Jayston's vivid portrayal, to see how small the part is, in action if not in lines. He doesn't even get to go on location.

Colin Baker's Doctor is also largely not that well served here. He only has one scene with his companion, and in that the latter is an illusion (the real Melanie never leaves the courtroom). Saward's *Revelation of the Daleks* also minimized the Doctor's involvement, in terms of both onscreen appearance and plot motion, and when looking at this script it is hard not to think of his later comments about both Colin Baker and Bonnie Langford's suitability for **Doctor**

Who[185]. The Doctor's part is, as with almost all the other characters', largely reactive. He does save the day, by sacrificing himself – and as a conclusion to this serial, that deserves considerable praise – but outside this he has little to do. He fails to pick a lock, and has the plot explained to him by the Master.

Whereas Holmes' intention had been for the Master to present as the serial's ultimate villain, in Saward's finale he becomes, in effect, the anti-hero of the whole piece. This does build on Part 13, where it is the Master's use of Glitz as a surprise witness and his revelation of the Valeyard's identity that cause the Doctor's trial to collapse. Here we are informed that these revelations have also prompted the High Council's resignation, making it impossible for the Valeyard to accomplish his own plan. It is also the Master who separately informs the Doctor and Inquisitor that the Valeyard has access to a genocidal weapon, allowing the Keeper and the Doctor to take action to try and avert catastrophe. It is even the Master who instructs Glitz to close the Time Vent once the Valeyard and the Doctor are trapped within it, in the process saving the universe.

---

[185] Most notably in 'The Revelations of a Script Editor', but also on other occasions. It is possible, even likely, that the minimising of the Doctor's role in many stories in the 1985 series is related to Saward's belief that Baker was not a suitable leading actor. The Bakers' immediately post-Saward scripts, for Parts 9 to 12, place the Doctor centre-stage throughout, and their version of Part 14 presents the Doctor as the central character, which Saward's arguably does not. Both Pip and Jane have often made clear their respect for Colin Baker's intelligence and admiration for his presence as an actor. It is very hard not to draw the obvious conclusions from these differing opinions and the scripts written by those who expressed them.

The Master is, overall, characterised in a manner more in line with post-2005 **Doctor Who** than the 1980s version, here presented as someone with whom the Doctor still has a vestige of friendship, and even affection. He also gets the script's best line when he informs the Doctor he has refused the High Council's attempt to commission him to kill the Doctor in order to defeat the Valeyard as it would 'ruin my anti-establishment image.' At the end of the episode the Master enthusiastically tries to involve Glitz in his plans for a universe without the Doctor, but nothing can alter the fact that the script gives the task of saving the universe to the Doctor's arch-enemy and another character introduced as a villain, who has in these two episodes both played a 'companion' role to the Doctor and been revealed as a 'business associate' of the Master's[186].

The Doctor and Melanie's aforementioned sole scene together is in many ways the centrepiece of the episode, figuratively and literally. It features the Doctor and an illusory Melanie becoming trapped within an endless corridor, in the process becoming loudly obsessed with figures of speech relating to circumlocution. That scene, Scene 8, was written by Saward for Bonnie Langford's audition for the part of Melanie, in 1985. It contains many phrases that are, frankly, difficult to say with any degree of feeling or conviction. Or indeed at all. Saward has indicated that he wanted to challenge Langford – about whose casting he was unconvinced – and that he was impressed by her reading of it opposite Colin Baker.

---

[186] Saward has said Glitz is 'a nice foil for the Doctor' in Part 13, something few would dispute. Which makes it odd that the characters are separated throughout his Part 14.

When he received Saward's Part 14, Baker remembered having performed that scene the year before, and has indicated that perhaps the inclusion of several pages of already-written material, which after all form a narrative cul de sac, indicated that Saward's heart was not in the task of writing Part 14[187]. This is possible, and Saward has acknowledged since that he was effectively mourning Holmes when he wrote this script[188], but the scene also ties into everything the script tries to accomplish thematically. It may be taken either as the cause of, or an excuse for, the script's extensive circular plot movement.

Doctor Who is, in popular parlance, a series that features 'running up and down lots of corridors'[189], and here Saward traps the Doctor and Melanie in an infinite corridor. Equally, adventure fiction is prone to circular plotting, and here Saward draws attention to that. **Doctor Who** is also a verbose programme, and Colin Baker's characterisation of the Doctor is, partially at Saward's instigation, a particularly verbose one. The scene feels like both an interrogation of the series and, perversely, Saward indulging everything he wants to do within it. It's the way the material is inserted into the

---

[187] Baker, Colin, 'Imitating Reality', DWM #206.

[188] 'I'd never experienced this feeling before, and there it was, and it's a terrible feeling, it gets in the way, you don't want to work very hard, you don't want to do anything very much, and I think that's what I was going through.'

[189] The sentiment is often expressed, but I have taken this phrase from **The Lenny Henry Show** transmitted 3 October 1985 and included on the second disc ('Mindwarp') of *The Trial of a Time Lord* DVD set. It featured a lengthy **Doctor Who** sketch that specifically spoofed the 1985 series of **Doctor Who**, rather than a generic idea of **Doctor Who**.

episode, via the Valeyard cackling about 'the most perfect geometric shape', and then resolved, with the Doctor simply realising and Popplewick shrugging off the failure to trap the Doctor, which doesn't work, rather than the scene itself.

It is, ironically, the literalism of how the scene is topped and tailed, rather than the dreamlike logic of the scene itself which fails. Holmes' Part 13 is flawed in many ways, but its 'surreal theme', to use Saward's term, does have its own nightmarish quality, a sense of unreality and unpredictability unusual for **Doctor Who**, which Saward's draft of that episode sustains. On the other hand in Saward's Part 14 the Victorian setting is simply that, another setting, where the Valeyard springs science-fiction traps while planning to execute a science-fiction master plan. It all feels rather ordinary.

Yet it shouldn't. The episode's central argument about, indeed its fixation on, the Valeyard's contract with the Time Lords is, if not surreal, then determinedly odd. That this contract could alter reality when 'lodged in the Matrix', regardless of what anyone wants, but have no power at all when not filed there, is as abstract a threat as anything in **Doctor Who**. While this is interesting, it is understandable that it is quickly superseded by the Valeyard's more traditional adventure-fiction threat of killing everyone with a made-up space weapon. (A threat which is also the Bakers' unconnected response to the need for an ending to the story, as if the narrative itself is pushing to be concluded in such a manner.)

Of course, comparisons such as this were impossible when the script was written, this draft preceding any notion of the Bakers' writing their own version, but they are somewhat irresistible in the

21st century, even when attempting to look at the script in isolation. This is the context the script exists in now. Few, if any, of those who read even a synopsis of it will not be familiar with the transmitted episode or its novelisation.

And that's significant. Saward's Part 14 is a penumbral version of the finale to the 1986 series of **Doctor Who**. It may be what was meant to be but, exactly like the Valeyard in the Bakers' replacement script, it's inhibited, unactualized. It's hemmed in by what happened instead. A frustrated shadow-self that never quite existed.

CHAPTER 5: PART 14 BY PIP AND JANE BAKER

Eric Saward's script for Part 14 is not in any way represented in the episode written by Pip and Jane Baker that was eventually made. The Bakers' script was not a rewrite of Saward's, in the way that Saward's Part 13 had been a rewrite of Holmes's. Nor did they work from any story material left in the production office which indicated what its contents were. Their script is a separate composition, produced over a few days, shortly after Saward withdrew his own draft from consideration for production.

Although writing for the 1986 series of **Doctor Who**, the Bakers were not party to the behind-the-scenes conflicts discussed in the preceding two chapters. They had been commissioned for Parts 9 to 12 after a chance meeting with Nathan-Turner in a lift at BBC Television Centre and, after being briefed by Nathan-Turner and Saward to produce an all-studio four-episode story in the style of Agatha Christie[190], and given the time constraints on the production, agreed to deliver the serial an episode a week. (They hand-delivered the scripts to Television Centre on Sundays and were then called by the **Doctor Who** production office after the script had been read on the following Monday, with notes on how to proceed.)

---

[190] Nathan-Turner may have had an eye on gaining the approval of Jonathan Powell, who had internally made clear his huge (and justified) admiration for the BBC's then in-production **Miss Marple** (1984-92), produced by George Gallaccio. Ironically, Gallaccio had been Nathan-Turner's predecessor as **Doctor Who**'s Production Unit Manager, the role Nathan-Turner had held on the series immediately before becoming its Producer in 1980.

Saward left his position as **Doctor Who**'s Script Editor after a meeting with the Bakers about the first two episodes of their Vervoid story.

> 'We started with Eric, and then he disappeared. John became the script editor and we just went on. All that John told us was that Eric had decided to go freelance and was doing the last episodes.'
>
> [Pip Baker][191]

They were also aware that the series' two-part finale was facing problems, thanks to earlier communication from Saward:

> 'Eric phoned us from home and he didn't give us all the details of why he'd left. He'd called us earlier to say that Bob Holmes was having terrible difficulties with episode 14 and that he felt he just couldn't write it'[192].

The pair, though, were not told the Valeyard's identity, or anything about the content of Parts 13 and 14[193]. Saward had also asked them to include scenes in their story where the Matrix seemed to lie, showing the Doctor onscreen behaving out of character, with the Doctor in the court disputing the Matrix's version of events, but were not told how this plot point would be played out in the

---

[191] Hearn, 'Writing Who'.

[192] Marson, 'Pip and Jane Baker'.

[193] It is impossible to know if the Valeyard's line 'Is it to be the Doctor's defence that he improves? This I must see!' from Part 9 was added to it after the Bakers saw the Script for Part 13. Certainly, though, it was recorded on the same day as the Trial Room scenes for Part 13, and Jayston's delivery takes full advantage of the irony, intended by the authors or not.

118

episodes after their own.

While they were also made aware that Holmes, whom they had never met, had died ('We didn't know him, but Eric was very upset and emotional about it'[194]), from their perspective at that point, following the acceptance of their script for Part 12, their active involvement in the then current series of **Doctor Who** was over. ('We were finished with *The Trial of a Time Lord*, we'd gone on to other things,' notes Pip[195].)

One afternoon, they were at home and the telephone rang, Jane answered it, and was surprised to discover Nathan-Turner on the other end of the line[196]:

> 'Jane had a rather strange conversation with John [...] He said, "There's a taxi on its way to you with a script in it. Read it tonight and come in the morning." And he wouldn't say any more.'[197]

> 'Jane and I assumed that someone had been rewriting our Vervoid story.'[198]

> [Pip Baker]

> 'But then [...] he said, "It's Part 13. I want you to read it and

---

[194] Baker, Jane, in Marson, 'Pip and Jane Baker'.

[195] Speaking on the Part 14 DVD commentary.

[196] Pip Baker recalls that this phone call interrupted a horse race on which he had bet, and in which a horse called Dancing Brave came second. Given the meetings calendar and results of that turf season, Nathan-Turner must have called the Bakers at almost exactly 4:30pm on Wednesday 4 June 1986.

[197] Marson, 'Pip and Jane Baker'.

[198] Hearn, 'Writing Who'.

come in tomorrow morning." I asked him what for, and he said, "I don't want to discuss it any more, Jane. Would you please just read it and come in tomorrow morning and I'll explain it all to you." So the taxi turned up, and we read Bob Holmes's episode. We both thought it was fine, but couldn't imagine what may have happened in the end.'[199]

[Jane Baker]

'We still didn't know why we were reading it.'[200]

[Pip Baker]

The Bakers turned up at Nathan-Turner's office the next morning, and were surprised to discover a fourth person in the room, besides themselves and the Producer. Jane Baker in particular had expected an informal meeting involving coffee and the latest BBC gossip[201], and was surprised by Nathan-Turner's unusually subdued demeanour. The Producer told the Bakers that the unexpected person was a legal witness, who was there to minute the meeting.

Having explained the situation with the withdrawn Part 14[202] and

---

[199] Hearn, 'Writing Who'. I conjecture that it is this physical script, sent to the Bakers' home, that they worked from when writing the first half of their 1988 novelisation, explaining the book's nature as an expression of an interim draft.
[200] Hearn, 'Writing Who'.
[201] She made this point every time she was interviewed about this meeting (e.g. Marson, 'Pip and Jane Baker'; Hearn, 'Writing Who'; 'Trials and Tribulations'; 'The Making of *The Trial of a Time Lord* Part 4: "The Ultimate Foe"' (DVD extra)).
[202] An interesting side note is Pip Baker's 1987 recollection that Holmes had written '12 minutes of the last episode' (i.e. Part 14) before his death (Marson, 'Pip and Jane Baker'). This **must** be a

asked the Bakers to write a replacement episode, he went on to inform them that the cast were already in rehearsal, the sets and locations had already been chosen based on the withdrawn script and that he needed the replacement, should they agree to deliver it, within three days. 'I asked him what was supposed to happen and he said, "I can't tell you – that's why the observer is here."'

By his own account, Pip Baker in particular thought they had been placed in a ridiculous situation by the request. However, they had some experience of writing under pressure, and to such an extraordinary deadline, having worked on the Elstree-shot American series **The Pursuers** (1961-62), a job during which they were expected to produce a script every three days for a number of weeks, routinely writing for 18 hours a day between them.[203] Not rejecting the idea in principle, the Bakers went into Saward's now-vacated office, to develop ideas for a replacement script. Nathan-Turner suggested the three of them go for lunch, but the writers, if not the Producer, understood that time was of the essence. Nathan-Turner provided the Bakers with the photographs of the locations that Chris Clough had already chosen, based on Saward's Part 14, along with a list of cast and characters, and intended sets.

The first decision they made was that they would not rewrite or interfere with the draft of Part 13 as it stood, but would instead try and build a Part 14 of their own that followed the episode they had

---

misremembering or a recollection of a miscommunication. No other source suggest Holmes ever began writing Part 14, and his contribution to the shooting script of Part 13 constitutes around 12 minutes of material.

[203] Baker, Pip, Part 14 DVD commentary.

been given[204]. They emerged a few hours later with a rough idea, which Nathan-Turner professed to love. Their one condition for accepting the job was that they were allowed to blow up the courtroom set, having learned from cast and crew on the series that everyone involved was bored to tears with the large but restrictive and difficult to shoot set. Ultimately, it was the Bakers' affection for Nathan-Turner that swayed them into accepting the job. ('Well, it was a challenge, and John was pleading. And we liked John,' said Pip in 1993). Jane would later express a desire not to see what she saw as public money wasted on a series with no conclusion[205], while both were aware that Nathan-Turner had no-one else to turn to should they refuse[206].

---

[204] Hearn, 'Writing Who'. This contention is borne out by comparing the various drafts of Part 13. The very small number of changes made to Part 13 in early June are related to linking its opening moments to the end of Part 12, and fall within the remit of basic script editing.

[205] Hearn, 'Writing Who'. 'Another thing both of us are conscious of,' noted Jane:

> 'not only on **Doctor Who** but on anything we spend hundreds of thousands of pounds on, I'm always conscious that there are hospitals needing scanners or schools needing new roofs. The BBC had already spent a lot of money on **Doctor Who** and we didn't want that to simply go down the drain.'

The Bakers had first met in 1955 when Jane was secretary of the Hanger Lane Labour Party, and Pip had been sent from another constituency to act as an election agent for what was then a marginal constituency.

[206] Theoretically, he could have asked Philip Martin, who had written Parts 5 to 8, to write a replacement Part 14. Indeed, having participated in the original discussions about *Trial* a year earlier, he

The Bakers' concerns about taking the commission were both professional and creative. The episode had to provide a satisfactory climax to three months' worth of serial for the millions of people watching, but they were also aware that, should be it seen as substandard or inchoate, then it was still their names that would be onscreen, credited as writers. Jane Baker later noted that they could hardly insist on a caption explaining that they'd only had days to write the episode included as part of the credits[207]. The Bakers' routine as a writing partnership was for one or the other to write in longhand on paper while the other talked, meaning that in practice their three-day deadline was a day shorter. The third day would be needed to type the script up before it was sent to Nathan-Turner. In the end they delivered the script on Tuesday 10 June, five days (and not quite three full working days) after their initial meeting with Nathan-Turner on Thursday 5 June.

(The Bakers do recall being phoned by Saward during those three days. A brief conversation ensued in which they assured him that they had not seen, or been told the content of, his script, and that

---

might have been better placed to write a script quickly. Nathan-Turner may, though, have asked the Bakers first exactly because they had not been in that meeting, reducing the possibility of cross-contamination of ideas in which Saward might be able to claim copyright. Additionally, Martin had been brought to **Doctor Who** by Saward, and Nathan-Turner had initially been suspicious of the writer, best known for his series **Gangsters** and the **Play for Today** which gave rise to it, and his suitability for **Doctor Who**.

[207] In the end Part 14 would be Pip Baker's expressed favourite of the episodes the duo wrote for **Doctor Who** precisely because of the difficult nature of the task, and his consequent pride in accomplishing it. (Jane Baker was unsure if she preferred Part 14 or *The Mark of the Rani*.)

they had come up with their own ideas based on the final draft of Part 13[208].)

The script was accepted by Nathan-Turner and Clough, and then taken to the cast, who were rehearsing Part 13 at the BBC's Acton rehearsal rooms. There it was read, and proved to be overlong, containing roughly 38 minutes of material, some of which was able to be cut during rehearsals[209]. Given the time constraints on its composition, this may seem counterintuitive, but as the saying goes, 'I would have written a shorter letter, but I did not have the time'[210].

What are we to make of the Bakers' script, and the episode that resulted from it? Well, it could be said that that the remarkable thing about the Bakers' Part 14 is not that it is done **well**, but that it is done at all[211], and while that is a fair reflection of the extraordinary speed with which they produced it under difficult circumstances, it is also unfairly to damn it with faint praise. Written under greater time, but far less emotional, pressure than Saward's, it does manage to serve as a climax to ongoing plot threads which the Bakers had had no part in devising and which they were given no help in concluding.

There are three main points of plot and story similarity between Saward's and the Bakers' Part 14s, and all are easily understood as

---

[208] Part 14 DVD commentary.

[209] All the cut material is included in the Bakers' novelisation, *The Ultimate Foe*.

[210] 'Je n'ai fait celle-ci plus longue que parce que je n'ai pas eu le loisir de la faire plus courte' (Pascal, Blaise, *Lettres Provinciales* (1657).)

[211] To paraphrase Dr Johnson.

growing out of the previous 13 episodes. The first is that both feature an illusory Melanie, who initially appears only as a disembodied voice[212]. In Saward's script this is when a duplicate of the Doctor's companion tempts him into the Valeyard's 'perfect geometric shape' trap. In the Bakers', a faux Mel seems to take the Doctor from the Matrix back into the Courtroom, where the Inquisitor sentences him to death for his actions in wiping out the Vervoids.

Despite both scenes featuring fake Melanies, they are very different in form and function, even as both serve the story's overall surreal tone, and there is no real link between them. The Bakers' version, in which we pull back from the courtroom to see that what we have been watching is on the screen in the courtroom, is an effective commentary on, and pay off for, the repeated use of this camera move throughout the Trial. it also draws attention to how much of what we have seen on the screen has been faked by the Valeyard, and reiterates a key theme of the whole Trial, that of establishing a narrative over events. The layers of reality in the Matrix could be seen to reflect the constant redrafting and overwriting of these episodes: not only do we pull back from a scene to discover it isn't really happening, we're repeatedly told things we saw in earlier episodes didn't happen either. The metafictional squabble to establish a chain of events seems to seep into the whole story.

The second similarity is more interesting. Both versions of the

---

[212] The illusion calling to the Doctor from offscreen is not present in the Bakers' draft, only onscreen, and may be a cross-pollination from Saward's draft via director Chris Clough, who did see both versions.

episode feature an offscreen insurrection on Gallifrey being reported by the Keeper of the Matrix. In Saward's script, the High Council resigns once the revelations about the Doctor's Trial have been made public, which the Keeper worries will send Gallifrey into turmoil; whereas in the Bakers' episode, the Keeper informs the court that the High Council has been deposed, and that 'insurrectionists are running amok.' While this is a logical development, considering the Doctor's show-trial and how it develops across Part 13, there is a possible common root for the two similar moments.

Colin Baker has often recalled, and the rehearsal script for Part 1 bears him out, that the Doctor's status as President of Gallifrey, established in *The Five Doctors* and referred to as recently as *Timelash* (1985), was not even referred to in the first version of *The Trial of a Time Lord* that he read. Baker mentioned this omission to Saward, who provided lines stating that the Doctor had been deposed in absentia for 'wilfully neglecting [his] great office'. However, according to David Halliwell's notes, the Doctor's being deposed as Time Lord President, and the replacement of the High Council with a Soviet-style 'continuing committee' (possibly a gestalt hive-mind) formed part of the *Trial* season at its earliest conception, as discussed in summer 1985[213]. This intention is not carried through into the finished serial, where the High Council is more than once referred to as still being the ruling body of Gallifrey, but it is both odd and interesting that Saward, who must have known of, and may even have formulated, this intention, did not use it in his Part 14.

---

[213] Molesworth, 'Bob's Fantasy Factory'.

The third 'parallel' aspect is the Valeyard's intention to use a weapon of mass destruction at the story's climax. Such climaxes are common in **Doctor Who,** and what makes the comparison between Saward's and the Bakers' versions here interesting is the differences between them, rather than the similarities. While the Valeyard's intention to use the particle disseminator to murder the apparently distinguished Time Lords attending the Doctor's trial superficially resembles his plan with the Time Vent in Saward's draft, there are key differences. Saward's Valeyard's use of the Time Vent is a contingency plan, a response to the High Council's betrayal of him. The Bakers' Valeyard has, it seems, always intended to murder the court once he has gained the Doctor's lives, perhaps as a way of disposing of witnesses, perhaps merely as a way of wreaking havoc. (This script's Valeyard is, after all, a 'composite of every dark thought' the Doctor has had, a Hyde to his Jekyll, not simply a future Doctor. Such a character might decide to take murderous revenge on his own people.)

Equally, Saward's Doctor physically assaults the Valeyard to stop him using it, seemingly dying to save the universe, but leaves actually saving reality from the Time Vent to the Master and Glitz (and it's not as if he's even prearranged with them that they should do this – he is simply relying on them realising they can). In the Bakers' script the Doctor is told that it is impossible for him to disable the Valeyard's weapon, but he responds that if the Valeyard is capable of making the particle disseminator then, logically he, the Doctor, should be able to immobilise it, what with them being the same person[214]. Which is probably a better use of the

---

[214] This script's 'particle disseminator' (also referred to, oddly, as a 'megabyte modem' by Melanie) is perhaps not quite as effective a

Valeyard's unique nature as a villain than anything else in the story.

When the Valeyard is seemingly killed in the feedback from his own machine, the Bakers' also invoke, if not **Doctor Who** cliché, then 'the sort of thing that happens in **Doctor Who**', with villains killed by their own traps and plans as an incidental consequence of the Doctor trying to save others (and the Bakers' novelisation makes it clear that the Doctor would even save the Valeyard if he could[215]).

The Bakers' version of Part 14 also manages to build on aspects of Part 13 that Saward's draft did not, despite Saward's role in drafting Part 13. Saward's Part 14 not only gives Mr Popplewick little to do, it fails to advance or further gloss the Dickensian aspects of Part 13, despite Saward having introduced them. The Bakers, however, pick up the Dickensian referencing of Part 13, by bringing in dialogue from *A Tale of Two Cities* (1859) and having Melanie mention that novel's self-sacrificing hero, Sidney Carton, as well as by making greater use of Popplewick than Saward's version does[216].

The Bakers also return to the plot element of secrets stolen from the Time Lords' Matrix[217], which forms much of Holmes's Parts 1 to

---

threat a Saward's Time Vent, but it does the job, and despite the fairly hyperbolic terminology, its name, its ability to break down quarks and tau mesons, and its being inverted by a 'ray phase shift' were the result of a conversation with Pip's brother, a physicist working in weapons development.

[215] Baker and Baker, *The Ultimate Foe* p118.

[216] Pip Baker's father was a Dickens enthusiast, and the writer is, according to Jane on their Part 14 DVD commentary track, named after the protagonist of Dickens' *Great Expectations* (1861).

[217] It is presumably a coincidental, parallel extrapolation that Popplewick's possession of the 'master tape' of the Matrix secrets

4 and is referred to during the climactic revelations in Part 13, something that Saward's script does not do. The implication here is that the Ravolox 'caper' was one of the 'nice little tickles' during which Glitz was working for the Master, as referred to in Part 13. In doing so, they add an additional layer to the Master's plans, in the process revealing that Glitz knows the Master wants to kill the Doctor, and that he has been working for the Master since before he arrived in the courtroom. Glitz spends most of his scenes in this episode with the Master, the Doctor or both, and this builds more effectively on Glitz's entrance in Holmes's scripted scenes in Part 13 than Saward's draft does in making him the Valeyard's prisoner.

It is also arguable that the Master's announcement to the court that he is now in charge, because he has control of the Matrix, represents Holmes' notion that the Master, not the Valeyard, should be the serial's ultimate threat, more fully than Saward's anti-heroic portrayal of the character does.

That Glitz is employed by the Master and motivated by avarice, and the Master by a desire for conquest over his own people, and that they share a desire to retrieve the Matrix tapes, points to something else about this version of the episode. What the characters are doing and why they are doing it is much better defined than in Saward's version. Popplewick and the Keeper of the Matrix may both turn out to be the Valeyard, but they both have a purpose in the story. Popplewick, with a much expanded role compared to Saward's script, serves as a henchman to the

---

seems to follow on logically from his counterpart Bencray's reference to his hidden 'diddy box' in Holmes' original draft of Part 13?

Valeyard, at least before his identity is revealed, keeping the Valeyard himself offscreen some of the time and making his occasional appearances more powerful and threatening. He also serves a character purpose. As the Doctor notes when unmasking Popplewick, he is an example of the Valeyard sharing his other self's liking for literary quotation, pastiche, whimsy and even the grand guignol. The Keeper of the Matrix has less to do, but he ultimately has a function, revealed as some kind of puppet or projection or avatar of the Valeyard, to allow the archvillain to escape[218].

Melanie is a more headstrong character than in Saward's version. She dashes into the Matrix to help the Doctor, participates in the process of working out what the Valeyard's scheme is and contributes productively to his attempt to formulate a plan against it. Even the Inquisitor is seen to do more (although many of the character's lines in this episode are given to an illusory version) and when the Doctor suggests that she stand for President at the story's end – the implication being that she is essentially honest, and could help restore order and dignity to Gallifrey after the disgrace of the Doctor's trial – the Bakers even manage to bolt something resembling an arc and a purpose onto a nameless character who has, despite appearing in 14 episodes over three months, never had much to do beyond exposit.

While Saward's frustrations with bureaucracy are not particularly developed by the Bakers in their script, there is some space for the metafictional conceits that Holmes used in Part 13. Popplewick's

---

[218] This cliffhanger, far less effective than Saward's, was suggested to the Bakers by Nathan-Turner. They duly obliged by including it.

comment that of the six phases of the Matrix, 'the primitive phases one and two have been relegated to the archive' could be taken to refer to the BBC's mass junking of black-and-white first and second Doctor serials from the 1960s, especially considering that the prop that Popplewick and Glitz handle as they discuss the matter is the case for a two-inch videotape master. This is exactly the format upon which **Doctor Who** had long been recorded[219], and the kind of tape which would have been erased in large numbers in order to junk **Doctor Who**'s missing episodes. If we are to see the Fantasy Factory of these episodes, and of Holmes' intended title, as an avatar for the BBC, and Part 13's frustrations with bureaucracy as expressions of dissatisfaction with BBC internal procedures and politics, then this becomes even more pointed. This is especially so given the openness with which most of those involved in the 1986 series of **Doctor Who** acknowledge the 'Trial' concept as reflecting that the series itself was in effect on trial for its life following the abortive 1985 cancellation[220].

The Bakers' Part 14 is a more boisterous script than the draft it replaces. Its characters and their motivations are more clearly defined. It has more incident and more humour, and its climax offers catharsis of a kind (via a well-produced explosion) and vindication for the Doctor, as the charges against him are dismissed by the woman sitting in judgement over him. Unlike Saward's conclusion it could not be described as 'thin', either figuratively or,

---

[219] One-inch tape was introduced in 1984 with the recording of *Warriors of the Deep*.

[220] That this makes Glitz an avatar for **Doctor Who** fans is amusing, particularly given the character's greed and perfidy, but probably incidental.

given its extra length, literally.

Several minutes of that extra length were cut during rehearsals, and more in studio and on location, but even so the first edit of the final episode compiled by director Chris Clough was 33m long. Realising that the episode could not be cut down to 25m while retaining even a semblance of coherence, Nathan-Turner had to make a special application to Jonathan Powell for a transmission slot five minutes longer than that for which the episode had been commissioned. Powell, miraculously given the circumstances and the friction between them, consented after viewing the episode, agreeing, by Chris Clough's account, that three minutes could be lost, but removing eight would make it incoherent[221].

The episode was transmitted at a length of 29m 30s, the longest standard episode of **Doctor Who** produced in the 20th century.

In the immediate aftermath, some of the Bakers' fears about being held accountable for an unpopular episode that they had only had days to write proved grounded. They were invited to appear on the BBC discussion show **Open Air** on 15 December 1985. Viewers watching this programme were treated to the somewhat bizarre sight of presenter Pattie Coldwell saying that she hadn't understood *The Trial of a Time Lord* Part 14, while acknowledging that she hadn't seen any of the previous 13 episodes and had 'never got' **Doctor Who** as a programme before then.

Defending their work from both Coldwell and four members of the Liverpool **Doctor Who** Appreciation Society, the Bakers faced allegations both that the programme was too simple and 'run-of-

---

[221] Marson, Richard, 'Chris Clough'. DWM #135.

the-mill', and that it was too complex for fans, let alone casual viewers, to understand. Pip Baker in particular, argued back that too great a simplicity in **Doctor Who** was 'selling your audience short', that it was not a programme which allowed the audience to disappear to make a cup of coffee between scenes, and that the writers felt a duty to '[t]ry to make it demanding as far as the audience is concerned'.

Other fans felt differently (DWM readers voted Parts 13 and 14 their favourite 'segment' of *The Trial of a Time Lord* and the Bakers' Vervoid story second[222]), but the negative reaction the Bakers' defence of their own work received from both the fans present in the studio, and the programme's presenters, indicated a prevailing public attitude to **Doctor Who** considerably different from the affection that had been expressed in February 1985 when it had been threatened with cancellation.

The reasons for, and ramifications of, that change in attitude are worth looking at in parallel with other aspects of **Doctor Who** in 1986, and we'll do that in our next chapter. For the Bakers, the encounter was perhaps a rude awakening. Both of them commented that they had enjoyed working on the series 'until now', and that the letters they'd had from viewers who had taken the trouble to write to them had been uniformly positive.

If contact with fandom on television had brought the Bakers down to earth with a bump, for others involved in the show's writing and production, matters were about to become even worse.

---

[222] '23rd Season Survey Results', DWM 126.

CHAPTER 6: A VERDICT

The Trial of a Time Lord ends in a wrecked courtroom, the huge set that had appeared in every episode of the 1986 series, already shabby with overuse, trashed as part of the plot of Part 14. The screen-within-a-screen onto which the Doctor's adventures had been projected in an attempt to acquit both character and programme in the eyes of at least three different juries, hangs there broken and cracked. It's a surely-not-intentional symbol of how dysfunctional a programme which, three years before, had been loudly celebrating 20 years on the air, had become.

The week of Part 14's transmission was not, despite the long slog to get it to screen and the episode being the most watched instalment of the year, a point where anyone involved could look back on the last 22 months with much satisfaction. Colin Baker, an enthusiastic ambassador for a series he was proud to star in, in a role he harboured ambitions to play for longer than any actor before him, had already gone. When, on 28 October, Jonathan Powell asked Nathan-Turner not to renew Baker's contract, effectively firing the actor from the series, he made clear to the Producer that this directive had come from Michael Grade.

Nathan-Turner accepted the task, which he would later describe as the worst moment of his professional career, on the understanding that he himself would also be removed from **Doctor Who**, and given a different series to produce. This sort of higher managerial diktat, let alone the haggling over it was not, to put it mildly, in line with standard BBC procedures. David Reid called it a '[s]taggering, extraordinary thing to happen. The sixth floor just **didn't**, you know, get involved in casting.'[223]

But then the original cancellation decision of 1985, also taken by Grade and Powell, had not been in any way precedented either, and Nathan-Turner's response, while it saved his programme, had been even less so. In terms of a producer's relationship with his superiors, and their relationship with his programme, these were uncharted waters.

The half-conceptualised relaunch of the programme that followed the unorthodox events of March 1985 cost the series viewers[224], and the process of getting that relaunch on screen had destroyed the working relationship between the two men who had together been in control of **Doctor Who**'s creative direction for almost five years. It is tempting, easy and probably wrong, to personalise the dispute between Nathan-Turner and Saward, and to read that personal dispute as more extreme and long-gestating than it probably was – and because of this, much fan historiography has.

Many of those involved in **Doctor Who**'s production in this period, from regular cast members to freelance writers, claim to have been unaware of any overt tension between the two men during their

---

[223] 'Trials and Tribulations'.

[224] It is a matter of debate as to whether better scheduling, such as not being part of a BBC One autumn lineup seen to have collectively failed, would have helped *The Trial of a Time Lord* gain a larger audience, but the fact is that every single episode of the 1986 series of **Doctor Who** was watched by fewer people than every single episode of the 1985 series of **Doctor Who**, with the first 1986 episode watched by only slightly more than **half** the people who had tuned in to watch the first episode of 1985.

years on **Doctor Who**. Is this simply because they would not have been around them all the time? Possibly not. 'They were very different,' Nathan-Turner's secretary Sarah Lee – who would have been in the production office at least as often as either man – says:

> 'And I think that was probably good for **Doctor Who**. Eric thought about the stories and characters. He was very bright. They both had big personalities and took their jobs very, very seriously. They both had the programme at heart – they really pushed to do what they thought was good and right. They fought passionately for what they wanted in the programme. They could both be overdramatic at times. But if, as I later did, you work on feature films, you get a lot more hot air than ever went on in that office.'[225]

Saward himself recalled:

> 'We were both difficult, we both wanted our own way, we adjusted to one another over the years and at one stage we were getting on quite well. It was not an easy relationship, but I wouldn't say it was a disastrous relationship. We worked together five years, [and] we didn't have many stand-up rows, very few. Most of the time it was the routine of working together. John could be very efficient in getting things done and organising the production side of things. I wasn't right and he was all wrong, [it was] never like that. Being Script Editor and Producer is like a marriage. In all close relationships people bicker and get angry, so when I talk about John I remember most easily the negative side'.

---

[225] Marson, *JN-T* p241.

Shortly after Saward's resignation as Script Editor, and while he was writing his version of Part 14, Nathan-Turner wrote formally to his former colleague, thanking him for his contributions to **Doctor Who**, and saying he would miss his presence in the production office[226]. This was before the argument over the content of Part 14, the aftermath of which finally destroyed their working relationship, began in earnest. But what must be understood about that clash, which emerged shortly after that letter was written, is that the disagreement at the heart of it is one fundamentally rooted in their distinct roles on the episode: Scriptwriter and Producer.

Saward is trying to protect the story he is trying to tell. The nature of the Valeyard and of the serial's cliffhanger ending, which combine to make a challenging, yet arguably redemptive, statement about the nature of **Doctor Who** as a programme and the Doctor as a character, had always been part of the conception of the *Trial* series. By late 1986 they are, with most of the original scripts abandoned and Robert Holmes dead, virtually the only part of the serial's conception that remained intact. Of course Saward, a writer first and foremost, chooses this as his Golgotha. And rightly so.

> 'He wanted to end with a huge question mark but I was determined that after 14 weeks there should be a resolution. After **14 weeks** of the Trial, I felt we needed a vindication and a judgement at the end.'
>
> [John Nathan-Turner][227]

---

[226] BBC WAC T65/224, letter from Nathan-Turner to Saward, 22 April 1986.
[227] Interview with Bill Baggs.

Despite Saward's feeling that Nathan-Turner's demands for a resolution typified a liking for 'walk-down, happy pantomime endings'[228], the Producer's insistence that, at the end of a courtroom drama that had been onscreen for more than a quarter of a year, there had to be a verdict, is not without merit as an argument solely about storytelling. Nathan-Turner, though, had more than storytelling on his mind. He felt that a cliffhanger ending would give his superiors an 'excuse' to cancel **Doctor Who** for good:

> 'After the hiatus I wanted an ending that clearly implied that the show was back in business with no question mark hanging over its future. After the long transmission gap, I was keen to demonstrate that we were back on course.'[229]

Saward wrote to Nathan-Turner during their discussions about Part 14's ending, saying:

> 'If you think M Grade will take it off because of what I'm proposing, I think you're mistaken. He'll take it off, if he so chooses, however it ends. You could have "See you next Season" flashing in neon throughout the last episode and he would still cancel it. As you well know, it seems to be down to audience figures and his personal whim.'[230]

Rationally, Saward was correct. But what about the management of **Doctor Who** over the last two years had been rational? Almost nothing. The original cancellation had demonstrated a cavalier attitude to public money and BBC procedures, and BBC Drama's

---

[228] Saward, 'The Revelations of a Script Editor'.
[229] Nathan-Turner, *Memoirs*.
[230] BBC WAC T65/224, letter dated 26 May 1986.

response to the tabloid outcry that followed was, as Powell himself acknowledges, at best cowardly.

Nathan-Turner has been criticised for his fixation with **Doctor Who**'s publicity and its profile in the outside world, but here his interest in the series' public perception gives him an insight Saward seemingly lacked. The 'hiatus' did damage **Doctor Who**'s public standing. The initial response to the February 1985 cancellation was a flurry of media support for the series, but Grade's public comments in defence of that decision, drawing attention to ostensibly low ratings and criticising its creative direction, were effectively a preview of the so-called 'Ratner Effect'[231]. (A shift in attitude demonstrated by the hostile treatment of the Bakers on **Open Air**.)

In his dealings with Saward over the script for Part 14, Nathan-Turner had different priorities from the writer, the same priorities he had when dealing with the cancellation crisis 18 months before. He was trying to protect the programme he was making, and which he hoped would continue to be made, although he himself no longer wanted it within his charge. It may seem paranoid of him to consider the possibility that BBC drama might use a cliffhanger ending as an 'excuse' to end **Doctor Who**, but after 18 months of behind-the-scenes turmoil, and of unprecedented, and at times

---

[231] On 23 April 1991 Gerald Ratner gave a speech to the Institute of Directors at the Royal Albert Hall in which he described his family' jewellery chain's' products as 'total crap... cheaper than an M&S prawn sandwich and probably wouldn't last as long'. The widely reported remarks led to the almost total collapse of the company, the closure of hundreds of its shops and the chain's abandonment of the family name in an attempt to survive.

even vindictive-seeming action from higher management, it is surely understandable? Of course Nathan-Turner, a BBC staff producer, was principally concerned that the long-running series of which he has charge is not cancelled. And again, rightly so.

The impetus for *The Trial of a Time Lord* came, as we have seen, from the series' real-life 'trial'. The argument between Saward and Nathan-Turner is about the different kinds of vindication they are seeking for the programme, about the outcome of both trials. Saward's ending makes a redemptive statement about the series and its lead character, one which is demonstrated through plot and action but never stated outright. It seems to acknowledge recent creative errors, and by its lack of resolution admits to a once-inconceivable possibility – that **Doctor Who** may in fact be coming to an end.

What Nathan-Turner wants is a more literal vindication, in terms of both fiction and fact, with the Doctor having the charges against him dismissed, and a successful and recommissioned series absolving the production teams of the criticisms, insinuations and allegations that had been made against their output.

Both men want absolution through, and for, their work: Nathan-Turner from a verdict handed down, not by Lynda Bellingham's Inquisitor, but his BBC superiors and the viewing public. Saward too, has the viewing public in mind, but there is also his conviction that, as nothing either he or Nathan-Turner can do can affect **Doctor Who**'s chances of survival one way or the other, the best thing to do is trust in his own instinct as a writer.

Saward's versions of Parts 13 and 14 reflect not just this conflict, but the larger conflict, with Nathan-Turner and Saward on one side, and the more powerful Powell and Grade on the other. The frustration with bureaucracy. The continual going round in circles. The terrible uncertainty of his and Holmes's ending for the story, and perhaps the series itself. It is not a stretch to see life imitating art in the way the writer's explosive end to his association with television **Doctor Who** followed his failure to get his similar fictional ending accepted by Nathan-Turner[232].

Writer and Producer had, if not irreconcilable, then radically different, intentions and even needs – even before we acknowledge, as anyone dealing with these episodes must, the tragic circumstances of Robert Holmes's death, and Saward's admitted desire to protect the intentions of a much-admired colleague and friend who, let us be frank, had been dead for little more than a week when Saward finally withdrew his script. This must have affected all of his responses and actions, professional and personal, in the days leading up to that decision. Although we have spent thousands of words on it, the withdrawal of a script for an early-evening adventure series is a trivial matter in comparison.

> 'Eric had formed a close relationship with Robert Holmes and was understandably upset and very protective of someone who'd been a role model to him. Robert Holmes was an excellent writer. We never met, but all the stories one remembers, the great ones, were written by Robert Holmes. He was the Daddy. He formed a paternal

---

[232] It might be stretching the point, though, to see Saward's public criticisms of Nathan-Turner after his own departure, and following a meeting with Powell in which both aired their grievances about the Producer, as a further life-imitating-art reflection of how often the characters in these episodes change sides.

relationship with Eric. No small wonder that Eric was protective. Whatever issues I have with Eric Saward[233], I respect his relationship with Robert Holmes.'

[Colin Baker]

'I also regret [...] the way I left, it was me being a small child to a degree, I wasn't prepared to listen any more. I would like to have left cleaner, to wrap things up. Later I felt, 'Why did I feel so awful? Why didn't I stay?' and I realised I was in [...] mourning.'

[Eric Saward]

Given all this, it is very hard not to see wisdom in Colin Baker's feeling, as early as spring 1985, that for the series to reflect onscreen its offscreen troubles was not a particularly good idea.

When Saward acknowledges that, in their creative clashes, it wasn't a case of him being always completely right and Nathan-Turner being always completely wrong, he demonstrates how their final argument was a microcosm of how their creative partnership had always worked. It is, yes, surely true that had Grade or Powell felt able to cancel **Doctor Who** at the end of 1986, they would have done, regardless of the specifics of its content. But they did not. Given their shared dislike of the programme, not to mention the failure of the 'Trial' to capture audiences and critics, it is hard to

---

[233] Baker took offence at comments made by Saward, initially in his *Starburst* interview ('The Revelations of a Script Editor') but also subsequently, about the actor's suitability for, and performances in, the role of **Doctor Who**. Baker found this particularly egregious because Saward had visited Baker's home and been introduced to his family.

see why they did not. It can only have been because they felt that insufficient time had passed since the tabloid scandal prompted by their last effort to cancel the series, and they simply didn't want to go through all that again[234].

In the end, BBC Drama ordered 14 episodes of **Doctor Who** for 1987 before the final episode of *The Trial of a Time Lord* was completed, let alone transmitted, making the entire relationship-destroying argument between Nathan-Turner and Saward wholly, even tragically, moot.

In another irony, Grade's removal of Baker led the actor to sell his story to the same newspaper to which Nathan-Turner had leaked the cancellation news nearly two years before[235]. This provided more public and professional embarrassment for Grade, whose stewardship of BBC One was now seen as 'under siege'[236]. Before the end of 1987 Grade left the BBC entirely, having been at the corporation for less than three years, moving to Channel 4 where he worked, with considerable success, for a decade.

Even 20th-century **Doctor Who**, wounded as it was, outlived Michael Grade's ultimately brief tenure as Controller of BBC One, and it was Powell, a staff producer like Nathan-Turner four years earlier, who succeeded him in that powerful, managerial and ultimately not-quite-creative role. Despite both Grade and Powell's many achievements in television (and only the most churlish and

---

[234] It is **incredibly** telling in this context that the 1989 cancellation of **Doctor Who** was never formally announced as such.

[235] Carroll, Sue, 'Why I'll Never Forgive Gutless Grade, by Axed Dr Who'. *The Sun*, 6 January 1987.

[236] This perception was not attributable to his dealings with **Doctor Who**, but was not wholly unrelated to it.

partisan of **Doctor Who** aficionados would deny that they both have very many), their fractious, reluctant association with **Doctor Who**, a programme neither man liked or wanted to make, remains one of the most remarked-upon moments in either man's career.

Grade would find himself fielding questions concerning his brief involvement with **Doctor Who** for decades[237], and in 2002 would use his appearance on the BBC Two programme **Room 101** to banish **Doctor Who** (then not even in production) into the eponymous chamber containing the 'worst things in the world'[238].

There Grade would explain his original dislike for **Doctor Who** (then no longer in production) in easily graspable terms, saying that having seen *Star Wars* (1977), *Close Encounters of the Third Kind* (1977) and *ET: The Extra-Terrestrial* (1982), he could not take low-budgeted television science fiction seriously[239]. Jonathan Powell has separately noted that in 1985 the programme was made for little money and that the resources allocated to it would have to be tripled for it to reach its potential as a series[240], and this symmetry

---

[237] It is routinely brought up by interviewers talking to Grade, who remains a public figure in a way Powell does not.

[238] **Room 101** (1994-2007, 2012-), 15 April 2002. Grade did not solely blame the budget, implying a lack of skill on the part of those making the series on that budget was equally to blame.

[239] Grade, an excellent generator, refiner and repeater of interview soundbites, would manage to use almost exactly the same words when comparing 1985's **Doctor Who** unfavourably with the series' 21st-century revival when interviewed on BBC Radio 5 on 4 September 2008 ('Doctor Who Radio Int with Michael Grade BBC Radio 5, 9/4/08').

[240] 'Trials and Tribulations'; Marson, *JN-T*, pp240-250. It is not without irony that people intimately involved in the setting of

may indicate some of the thinking behind their original joint decision of 1985.

That decision, in practical terms a mere footnote in either's career, has as good a chance of being – fairly or not – what both men are remembered for, to exactly the same extent that **Doctor Who** is already Robert Holmes and John Nathan-Turner's posterity.

This is because **Doctor Who** – not the **Doctor Who** of 1985 or 1986, not even **Doctor Who** as a television programme, or as a 'national institution', but simply as an **idea**, as a fictional process for generating stories – is bigger than anyone ever involved in that process. Bigger than any of the individuals involved in the making of these episodes, regardless of whether they were on the sixth floor or the studio floor. This essential truth is something that Grade seems not to have grasped[241], and Powell may perhaps have

---

Doctor Who's budget should criticise it for looking cheap when the solution to this problem was within their gift.

[241] Or perhaps not **then**. It is worth noting that any dislike Grade had for the series was not so ingrained that he was unable to see the merit of the 2005 revival of **Doctor Who**. He is on record praising its quality and its creative success where, in his opinion, previous iterations of the programme had failed ('Michael Grade: "I Think The BBC Has Become Too Bureaucratic"'.). The very cynical may choose to see Grade's praise of 21st-century **Doctor Who** as a way of defusing a decades-long line of questioning that had suddenly become more pointed, but tellingly he praised the programme not only during his tenure as BBC Chairman (2004-06) but also after it, when he had once more returned to commercial broadcasting and had no professional reason to praise the programme, as he did in 2005, as 'real value for money for our licence fee payers' (Deans, Jason, 'Doctor Who Finally Makes the Grade').

had a sense of, but resented. Its ability to distract from other BBC drama programmes that Powell thought more deserving of attention was perhaps one of the causes of his dislike of the programme[242]. If so, the fact that the programme could attract more publicity by being cancelled and reprieved than others could by simply existing in a form he considered successful must have frustrated him yet further. Powell spent five years as Controller of BBC One, with **Doctor Who**'s eventual demise in 1989 happening under his successor as Head of Drama, Peter Cregeen[243].

The months since that first, shocking meeting with Powell on 25th February 1985 had seen **Doctor Who** lose half its yearly screen-time, its Script Editor, its Producer, and its star, as well as the death of its most admired writer. But there was to be another twist in the sorry tale. On 28 November 1986, despite previous assurances to

---

[242] Ken Riddington, formerly the producer of **Tenko** (1981-84), a friend of Nathan-Turner's and by then Acting Head of Drama Series and Serials under Powell, told Nathan-Turner that he had made such an industry of **Doctor Who** that no other producer in the department was prepared to take it on. Powell's period as Head of Department saw productions such as **Edge of Darkness** (1985), **A Very Peculiar Practice** (1986-88), **The Singing Detective** (1986) and **The Monocled Mutineer** (1986), and the start of the long-running **Lovejoy** (1986, 1991-94). *A Murder is Announced*, the third serial in BBC One's **Miss Marple**, of which Powell was hugely proud, was transmitted on 28 February and 1-2 March 1985, the exact span of the 'cancellation crisis'. Perhaps BBC Drama had anticipated this period as being filled with bouquets rather than brickbats?

[243] Powell's time at the BBC ended when he found himself at the centre of another tabloid furore, held responsible for the costly failure of the soap **Eldorado** (1992-93). He moved to the uniquely undistinguished ITV franchisee Carlton, before leaving television production and entering academia.

contrary, Nathan-Turner was informed by Powell that he would, in fact, have to produce the 1987 series of **Doctor Who**, and that his only alternative was to leave the BBC altogether[244]. Again, as he had two years before, Nathan-Turner chose not to resign from the BBC. This was a situation which his friend Colin Baker rather generously made clear he understood[245].

Now **Doctor Who**'s re-appointed reluctant Producer was faced with a situation where he had no star, no script editor and no scripts,

---

[244] A possible explanation for both Powell's originally agreeing to Nathan-Turner's request, and then rescinding that agreement, and Grade's request that BBC Drama not renew Colin Baker's contract, may lie in the fact that Grade had been in contact with Sydney Newman, **Doctor Who**'s creator and Powell's distant predecessor as BBC Head of Drama, and had asked Newman to write a critique of then-current **Doctor Who**. Newman duly did this, but insisted that if any of the ideas were taken up he would wish to produce the series. Grade and Powell's enthusiasm for Newman's ideas cooled once they had read his proposals, but it may be that they were clearing the decks for Newman. Given that media pressure ensured **Doctor Who** had to be made, putting the series' creator in charge of another revamp would have both been good publicity and ensured no one could accuse BBC drama of not taking relaunching **Doctor Who** seriously. Timing is key here: Baker's contract would have had to be renewed in the period where discussions with Newman were ongoing. As Newman had his own, firm, ideas about casting (the return of Patrick Troughton, followed by a female Doctor after two series), picking up Baker's option might have meant paying the actor for a series for which he was not required for the second time in three years. (Newman, Sydney, *Head of Drama: The Memoirs of Sydney Newman*.)

[245] In his *Memoirs* Nathan-Turner describes Baker as 'A good man, a good actor and a good friend,' with particular reference to this period of his own career.

and roughly 72 working days to get the first serial of the 1987 series into studio. Nathan-Turner noted in his *Memoirs* that 'Jonathan said something quite brief like "You'll cope," as I was shown out. Under my breath I said something equally brief.' In the end, the script for that serial (*Time and the Rani*) would also be supplied by Pip and Jane Baker, on whom he had now come to rely and who had thus far not let him down, supplying workable and producible scripts with virtually no notice[246].

There was another reason too, although it may never have entered Nathan-Turner's head, to entrust yet another enforced relaunch of **Doctor Who** to the Bakers. Their version of Part 14, for all its extemporised nature, displays both an energy and, significantly, a faith in the future viability of **Doctor Who**, both as a programme and as a character, that is almost entirely absent from the exhausted and demoralised Saward's richer, but essentially despairing conclusion.

---

[246] This decision, and the fact that Parts 13 and 14 were produced before parts 9 to 12, meant that in production order the Bakers wrote nine episodes of **Doctor Who** in a row – *The Trial of a Time Lord* Parts 14 and 9-12, and *Time and the Rani*. While this is not a record (*The War Games* represents Malcolm Hulke and Terrance Dicks co-writing 10 in a row), Nathan-Turner's reliance on the Bakers does create a usually neglected, distinct 'era' of the series where, after the departure of Saward and before the arrival of Andrew Cartmel, the pair were the de facto script editors and sole writers of **Doctor Who** for several months, and effectively in control of the series' creative direction. It is also worth noting that Parts 9 to 14, of which they wrote five-sixths, were the best-reviewed instalments of the 1986 series.

With *The Trial of a Time Lord* over, the Doctor and his friend were off to other adventures.

APPENDIX 1: TITLE FIGHT

The 1986 series of **Doctor Who** consisted of a single 14-episode serial with the onscreen title *The Trial of a Time Lord*. The decision to frame the series as a single serial, with one title, was taken relatively late in its production, and superseded a previous intention to have a series which, while (broadly) consisting of the same episodes, would have been credited onscreen as a series of four or five separate serials.

The television programmes transmitted as *The Trial of a Time Lord* Parts 1 to 4 and Parts 5 to 8 were given ostensibly final titles before the policy was changed. They were 'The Mysterious Planet' and 'Mindwarp' respectively, and these titles appear on some scripts as well as some commissioning documents. (Earlier 'working titles' had included 'Wasteland' for the former and 'Planet of Sil' for the latter.)

'The Mysterious Planet' and 'Mindwarp' are also distinct productions, despite some shared sets and cast. They had separate BBC production codes ('7A' and '7B' respectively'), separate crews, separate budgets, different writers and different directors.

However, by the time 1986's final six episodes came to be recorded Nathan-Turner had already changed his mind, in part because the publicity surrounding '**Doctor Who**'s longest ever story' could be used to distract from or deflate the unfortunate truth that the 1986 series was the shortest run of **Doctor Who** yet made. Thus 'final' titles weren't arrived at for these episodes, for the simple reason that they were never required.

There is another complication. Parts 9 to 14 constitute a single production ('7C') under a single director (Chris Clough), with a single budget and shared resources. (For example, the Trial Room scenes for Parts 9 to 12 were shot with those for Parts 13 and 14, and on the same day, whereas those for Parts 1 to 4 and Parts 5 to 8 were shot separately from each other, within their respective production dates).

This 'single production' seems to have been the intention even when it was possible they would constitute three separate two-part stories from three different writers (see 'Chapter 1: On Trial'). Thus whether '7C' / *The Trial of a Time Lord* Parts 9 to 14 constitutes one story or two, or whether it is merely a component of another, larger story is frankly a matter of interpretation, depending on which criterion matters the most to the individuals discussing the material.

Titles did become required **after** transmission, however, when novelisations of the 1986 series (split into Parts 1 to 4, 5 to 8, 9 to 12 and 13 to 14) were produced by Target Books, the company which had been publishing adaptations of **Doctor Who** television serials since 1973. For the first eight episodes, the abandoned 'final' titles were pressed into service. The novelisation of Parts 9 to 12 was titled *Terror of the Vervoids* on publication in 1987, a name with no basis in production office documentation.

Jane Baker later commented that 'Terror of the Vervoids' was 'the title WH Allen wanted'[247], and that she and her husband always referred to the story as simply 'The Vervoids'. Crucially she notes, 'They [the BBC] didn't want titles for the *Trial* stories.'

---

[247] Hearn, 'Writing Who'.

It's not hard to imagine the more dramatic title springing from then **Doctor Who** books editor Nigel Robinson, a fan of the series who would inevitably have been familiar with *Terror of the Autons* (1971) and *Terror of the Zygons* (1975).

The Bakers' novelisation of Parts 13 and 14 was published under the title *The Ultimate Foe*. Unlike 'Terror of the Vervoids' this title does have a basis in production documentation, but it is the title given to Parts 9 to 12, the Bakers' 'The Vervoids' (i.e. episodes 1 to 4 of production '7C') on the commissioning document dated 6 March 1986.

'The Ultimate Foe' is a plausible title for a serial which in theory pits all animal life against all vegetable life, but it is a far more suitable title for a story in which the Doctor battles an evil version of himself. It is this, as much as its use on the novelisation of Parts 13 and 14, and on their subsequent DVD release, that has led it becoming their de facto title.

It is not impossible to believe, knowing that the four episodes the Bakers had been commissioned to write would form part of a single production ('7C'), that the title given them at this point referred to the whole six episodes, not the Bakers' (then anticipated) four out of six. Nevertheless, some publications now refer to Parts 9 to 12, rather than 13 to 14, as 'The Ultimate Foe' in the interests of reflecting the commissioning document. Does this leave us without a 'title' for Parts 13 and 14? No. Parts 13 and 14 were commissioned from Robert Holmes as 'Time Inc' on 4 February 1986, and this is pressed into service to fill the gap.

However, the draft Holmes delivered of Part 13 is titled '**Doctor Who** – Part 13 – The Fantasy Factory' on page 1, indicating that for

Holmes, at least, the title had changed by this point. This makes sense, as 'Time Inc' was extremely unlikely to have survived to screen, even had the decision to transmit the season under a single title never been made. Not only has the fictional organisation to which the title refers become 'The Fantasy Factory' by the earliest script for Part 13 available to us (and remains so in the transmitted programme) but the obvious resemblance to the real life organisation Time Inc, which had existed since the 1920s and which owns *Time* magazine, would never have made it past BBC standards.

Therefore, while it is inarguable that Parts 13 and 14 were commissioned as 'Time Inc', to insist on referring to them as such is a misplaced pedantry, rather than accuracy. 'Time Inc' is not their title, and if accuracy is to be insisted on, we are required to refer to them as *'The Trial of a Time Lord* Part Thirteen' and *'The Trial of a Time Lord* Part Fourteen', which accords with both onscreen credits and the final draft scripts.

The cover of this book bows to convention in labelling the two episodes with which it deals 'The Ultimate Foe'. This is a matter of **Black Archive** house style, and is done in deference to their DVD release referring to them as such both on its jacket and in all supplementary and documentary material, rather than because it is accurate or the author's own personal preference. As such the term is avoided within the text of this volume, except in this Appendix and within direct quotation.

APPENDIX 2: EFFECT AND CAUSE

The penultimate scene of *The Trial of a Time Lord* sees the Doctor and Melanie depart the courtroom together in the TARDIS. While a reassuring statement of 'business as usual' for **Doctor Who**, this is, from a story perspective, very odd indeed.

Part 9, Melanie's first appearance, presents her as a companion from the Doctor's own personal future, someone whom the Doctor sitting in the dock has never met. When Part 13 brings her to the Trial Room, this is, from his perspective, his first ever meeting with her. From hers she has already met him for the first time (she recognises him) in what must have de facto been a different situation. In Part 14 she is able to comment from memory on events on board the *Hyperion III*, indicating that she has experienced the adventure with the Vervoids, something that the Doctor alongside whom she is fighting the Valeyard has not.

When they leave together at the end of the story, indicating a desire to share further adventures, the result is inherently paradoxical. This paradox is compounded by the Doctor's regenerating into another form in the first scene of the next **Doctor Who** serial. (Indeed, a viewer could be forgiven for believing the TARDIS is hijacked, and then crashes on Lakertya, leading to the Doctor's regeneration immediately after leaving the Trial Station, and there is little onscreen to dispute such an interpretation[248].)

---

[248] The Doctor and Melanie are wearing different clothes, but the implication of the position of the Doctor's prone body in *Time and the Rani* episode 1 is that he has fallen off the very exercise bike that Melanie demands he get back onto at the end of *The Trial of a Time Lord* episode 14.

John Nathan-Turner may have intended to show the Doctor meeting Melanie for the first time in the 1987 series[249], indicating that 'future' Melanie and 'present' Doctor parted company between series, and then abandoned this intention when the forced recasting of the series lead made this impossible, but onscreen the paradox of *The Trial of a Time Lord*'s penultimate scene is never resolved.

There is a kind of precedent within **Doctor Who** for exactly this kind of unresolved paradox, however. The situation is analogous to Sarah Jane Smith's adventuring with the Third Doctor in *The Five Doctors*. While the Doctor, merely by being played by Jon Pertwee, is explicitly from before the events of *Planet of the Spiders* (1974), the Sarah Jane he meets in the Death Zone has already experienced those events, and many others in the presence of his successor. At the end of *The Five Doctors* Sarah and the Pertwee Doctor also leave together in the TARDIS (as do Richard Hurndall's first Doctor and an older Susan Foreman, and the Patrick Troughton Doctor and an older Brigadier, who has met his three subsequent incarnations).

No-one, however, assumes that any of these characters will stay together and have subsequent adventures. Despite no indication onscreen that anything has happened other than three Doctors leaving Gallifrey in their own TARDISes, fan historiography assumes that Sarah, the Brigadier and Susan are automatically (or inherently?) returned to where they 'should' be ('our proper place in time and space' as the Davison Doctor puts it onscreen) rather

---

[249] Whether a casual viewer would have been more confused than reassured by seeing the Doctor meet for the first time someone they had seen him travelling with on television is a matter for debate.

than the older versions of 'their' Doctors being responsible for taking them home. This is of course in part because we largely do not subsequently see the characters together (no one, as far as I am aware, has ever suggested that the Pertwee Doctor and Sarah Jane of the 1993 radio serial *The Paradise of Death* or the same year's charity special *Dimensions in Time* are the temporally mismatched pair who leave Gallifrey in *The Five Doctors*[250]).

Pip and Jane Baker's novelisation of the last two episodes of *The Trial of a Time Lord* presents a simple, elegant 'out' from the paradox, one which builds on *The Five Doctors*'s implications (or fan assumptions about them). Immediately after leaving the Trial Station, the TARDIS, remote-controlled by the Time Lords, travels to the planet Oxyveguramosa. There Melanie walks out of the TARDIS and into another one that has appeared beside it. This one contains a Doctor who's 'caught up' with their joint experiences[251]. While effective, based on precedent within **Doctor Who**, and charmingly done, this resolution is never even referred to onscreen in subsequent television **Doctor Who**. But then neither is the paradox the epilogue is there to resolve.

Or is it? In the third episode of *Dragonfire* (1987), transmitted almost exactly a year later, Melanie decides to leave the Doctor and, bizarrely, travel with Sabalom Glitz. The Doctor, now played by

---

[250] Curiously the Pertwee Doctor and Sarah Jane Smith appear together in four ex post facto 'reunion' stories: *The Five Doctors*, *The Paradise of Death*, *Dimensions in Time* and *The Ghosts of N-Space* (radio, 1996) and only five serials in the 1974 series of **Doctor Who**, making the pairing almost as frequent as a nostalgic return as it was in situ.

[251] Baker, Pip, and Jane Baker, *The Ultimate Foe*, pp124-26.

Sylvester McCoy, responds to her announcing that she is leaving in a curious manner that seems to reference the paradox of her arrival.

DOCTOR

That's right, yes, you're going. You've been gone for ages. You're already gone, you're still here, just arrived, I haven't even met you yet. It all depends on who you are and how you look at it. Strange business, time.

MELANIE

Goodbye, Doctor.

DOCTOR

I'm sorry, Mel. Think about me when you're living your life one day after another, all in a neat pattern. Think about the homeless traveller and his old police box, with his days like crazy paving.[252]

The lines above were not deliberately written to resolve or refer to the end of *The Trial of a Time Lord*. They were, in fact, part of an audition script for actors screen-testing for the role of the Doctor in the 1987 series, written by Andrew Cartmel, Eric Saward's successor as **Doctor Who**'s Script Editor. They were pressed into service in the final episode of *Dragonfire*, at short notice when Bonnie Langford decided to leave **Doctor Who**, in part because Sylvester McCoy admired what Cartmel had written and wanted it to be used in a televised episode.

Yet these lines do work as an oblique reference by the Doctor

---

[252] *Dragonfire* episode 3.

himself to Melanie's peculiar relationship, temporally speaking, to him. An acknowledgment of the paradox that, if only what is seen onscreen is taken into account, they have experienced different, incompatible versions of their first meeting. The mere fact that *Time and the Rani* begins with the TARDIS being hijacked by another Time Lord, the Rani, may provide a story justification for this paradox. The hijacking prevents the TARDIS from taking Melanie home, and during that hijack the Doctor regenerates. History changes. Knowing that this has happened and that the paradox can no longer be resolved, the Doctor simply continues to travel together with Melanie, despite having different memories of how and when they met[253], simply because he wants to. (She and the Colin Baker Doctor are the first Doctor-companion pairing of the 80s who seem to genuinely enjoy each other's company onscreen, and her relationship with the McCoy Doctor is, if anything, more affectionate.) It's an example of art imitating life. Bonnie Langford was never meant to star alongside Sylvester McCoy, because Colin Baker had no intention of leaving **Doctor Who**. Melanie was meant to travel with the Sixth Doctor, but the events of *The Trial of a Time Lord* (in which they are **both** 'taken out of time') and *Time and the Rani* rewrite their history in relation to each other, and irreversibly.

20th-century **Doctor Who** rarely uses such ideas within its plots, but it is interesting to acknowledge what may be one of its few, perhaps accidental, examples. After all, 21st-century **Doctor Who**

---

[253] Maybe the McCoy Doctor nips to the *Hyperion III* and has Professor Lasky arrested before take off, solving the problem with the Vervoids before it starts. This would not be out of character for his Doctor as portrayed in the 1988 and 1989 series of **Doctor Who**.

has several characters whose relationship with the Doctor has led to the rewriting of their own personal history[254]. A redheaded companion who meets the Doctor in the wrong order, and then stays around when history changes, despite them having different memories of how they first met? That's Karen Gillen's Amy Pond. But, probably more by accident than design, Bonnie Langford's Melanie got there first.

---

[254] While the adult Amy Pond clearly met the Doctor and decided to travel with him, it is impossible to imagine that the events of *The Eleventh Hour* (2011) transpired exactly as they are seen onscreen in the restored reality where Amy grew up with two loving parents. Time has been rewritten, and the Doctor and Amy must remember different, and sometimes multiple, versions of reality – as is acknowledged in the bonus DVD minisode 'Night and the Doctor: Good Night' (2011).

APPENDIX 3: SCENE BREAKDOWNS (PART 13)

1. Holmes

Position in Script	Designation	Setting	Content
1	Telecine 1	Ext. Space	Model shot of station, single casket arrives.
2	Scene 1	Int. Trial Room	Court argument
3	Scene 2	Int. Corridor	Glitz emerges from casket alone.
4	Scene 3	Int. Trial Room	Glitz enters court. Valeyard revealed to be Doctor. Cross examination of Glitz. Valeyard flees.
5	Scene 4	Int. Corridor	Valeyard enters the Matrix. Doctor and Glitz give chase.
6	Telecine 2	Ext. Narrow Alley	Doctor and Glitz arrive in Matrix London together, Glitz gives Doctor note from Master, they hail a cab to Fantasy Factory.
7	Scene 5.	Int. Cab	Doctor-Glitz discussion.

8	Telecine 3	Ext. Street	Cab driver revealed to audience as Valeyard.
9	Scene 6	Int. Cab	Cab crashes.
10	Telecine 4	Ext. Street	Doctor and Glitz meet Bencray. Enter Fantasy Factory.
11	Scene 7	Int. Trial Room	Master insists to Inquisitor that the Doctor's trial was rigged.
12	Scene 8	Int. Anteroom	Doctor and Glitz meet second Bencray. Sign contracts. Leave.
13	Telecine 5	Ext. Street	Doctor and Glitz separated. Doctor witnesses murder. Is drowned by Duke and Stephens.

2. Holmes / Saward

Position in Script	Designation	Setting	Content
1	Telecine 1	Ext. Space	Model shot of station. Two caskets arrive. (This Telecine and Scene 1 switched in editing.)

2	Scene 1	Int. Trial Room	Court argument. (This scene and Telecine 1 switched in editing.)
3	Scene 2	Int. Corridor	Glitz and Melanie emerge from caskets. They meet, argue, decide to enter courtroom.
4	Scene 3	Int. Trial Room	Glitz and Mel enter court. Cross-examination of Glitz. Valeyard revealed to be Doctor. Valeyard flees.
5	Scene 4	Int. Corridor	Valeyard enters the Matrix. Doctor and Glitz give chase.
6	Telecine 2 / OB 1	Ext. Narrow Alley	Doctor arrives in Matrix London alone. Is attacked by hands in barrel. Glitz arrives, gives Doctor note from Master.
7	Scene 5	Int. Trial Room	The Master confirms that Peri did not die on Thoros Beta.
8	Telecine 3 / OB 2	Ext. Alley	Doctor persuades Glitz to help him. They enter the Fantasy Factory.
9	Scene 6	Int. Trial	Master insists to

		Room	Inquisitor that the Doctor's trial was rigged.
10	Scene 7 / OB 3	Int. First Clerk's Office	Doctor and Glitz meet Junior Mr Popplewick.
11	Scene 8 / OB 4	Int. Second Clerk's Office	Doctor and Glitz meet Senior Mr Popplewick. Sign contracts. Leave.
12	Telecine 4	Ext. Mud Flats	Doctor emerges onto beach alone. Is dragged into ground by hands.

ACKNOWLEDGEMENTS

I am indebted to Ed Stradling, Richard Molesworth and especially Richard Bignell for allowing me access to unpublished interviews and unique documents, to the British Library and the BBC Written Archive at Caversham (especially Samantha Blake) for assistance in research, and Paul Cornell and Richard Marson for permission to quote from their published work. I would like to thank Gareth Roberts and Jonathan Morris for their encouragement in tackling these particular episodes, Steffan Alun, Stuart Ian Burns, Mark Clapham, Ralf Collie, Gemunu Cooray, Saliya Cooray, Swyrie Cooray Smith, Jonn Elledge, Clayton Hickman, Ed Jefferson, Toby Longworth, Lance Parkin, Gordon Ridout and Eddie Robson for allowing already inevitable conversations about **Doctor Who** to turn back to these instalments over and over again, and all of the above for insights gained during those conversations.

BIBLIOGRAPHY

Books

Anon, *The String of Pearls: A Romance*. London, Salisbury Square, 1850.

Baker, Pip and Jane, *Doctor Who: The Mark of the Rani*. **The Target Doctor Who Library** #107. London, WH Allen, 1986. ISBN 9780426202325.

Baker, Pip and Jane, *Doctor Who: The Trial of a Time Lord – The Ultimate Foe*. **The Target Doctor Who Library** #131. London, WH Allen, 1988. ISBN 9780426203292.

Conan Doyle, Arthur, *The Penguin Complete Sherlock Holmes*. 1887-1927. London, Penguin Books Ltd, 2009. ISBN 9780141040288.

Dickens, Charles, *The Posthumous Papers of the Pickwick Club*. 1837. *The Pickwick Papers*, London, Penguin, 2000. ISBN 9780140436112.

Dickens, Charles, *A Christmas Carol in Prose: Being a Ghost Story of Christmas*. 1843. *A Christmas Carol and Other Christmas Writings*, London, Penguin, 2003. ISBN 9780140439052.

Dickens, Charles, *Little Dorrit*. 1857. London, Penguin, 2003, ISBN 9780141439969.

Dickens, Charles, *A Tale of Two Cities*. 1859. London, Penguin, 2003, ISBN 9780141439600.

Howe, David J, Mark Stammers and Stephen James Walker, *The Sixth Doctor*. **Doctor Who: The Handbook**. London, Virgin Publishing, 1993. ISBN 9780426204008.

Kaplan, Morris B, *Sodom on the Thames: Sex, Love, And Scandal in Wilde Times*. New York, Cornell University Press, 2005. ISBN 9780801436789.

Knight, Stephen, *Jack the Ripper: The Final Solution*. Edinburgh, Chambers Harrap, 1976. ISBN 9780245527241.

Marson, Richard, *JN-T: The Life and Scandalous Times of John Nathan-Turner*. Reigate, Miwk Publishing Ltd, 2013. ISBN 9781908630131.

Marter, Ian, *Doctor Who and the Ark in Space*. **The Target Doctor Who Library** #139. 1977. London BBC Books, 2012. ISBN 9781849904766.

Martin, Philip, *Doctor Who: Trial of a Time Lord – Mindwarp*. **The Target Doctor Who Library** #139. London, WH Allen, 1989. ISBN 9780426203353.

Molesworth, Richard, *Robert Holmes: A Life in Words*. Tolworth, Telos Publishing Ltd, 2013. ISBN 9781845830915.

Moore, Alan, and Eddie Campbell, *From Hell*. 1999. London, Knockabout Comics 2000. ISBN 9780861661411.

Newman, Sydney, with contributions by Graeme Burk, *Head of Drama: The Memoirs of Sydney Newman*. Toronto, ECW Press, 2017. ISBN 9781770413047.

Pascal, Blaise, *Les Provinciales, ou les Lettres escrites par Louis de Montalte a un provincial de ses amis & aux RR PP Iesuites: sur le sujet de la Morale & de la Politique de ces Peres*. Cologne: Pierre de la Vallee, 1667.

Perry, Robert, and Mike Tucker, *Matrix*. **Doctor Who**. London, BBC

Books, 1998. ISBN 9780563405962.

Roseberry, Lord, *Pitt*. London, Macmillan, 1891.

Saward, Eric, *Doctor Who: Attack of the Cybermen*. **The Target Doctor Who Library** #138. London, WH Allen, 1989. ISBN 9780426202905.

Periodicals

The Daily Telegraph.

'"Doing a Ratner" and Other Famous Gaffes'. 22 December 2007.

Lee, Harvey, 'BBC cash curbs grounds Dr Who'. 28 February 1985.

Lee, Harvey, 'BBC Buys £¾m Mini-Series after Dr Who Decision'. 2 March 1985.

The Daily Mail.

Donovon, Paul. 'Dr Who Down-Graded!'. 28 February 1985.

Donovon, Paul, 'Angry BBC Viewers Begin Here'. 1 March 1985.

Honan, Corinna, 'Grade: Why the Doctor Had to God'. 2 March 1985.

Doctor Who Magazine (DWM). Marvel UK, Panini, BBC, 1979-.

'23rd Season Survey Results'. DWM #126, cover date July 1987.

Baker, Colin, 'Imitating Reality'. DWM #206, cover date November 1993.

Cook, Benjamin, '"He Never Gives In And He Never Gives Up... He is Never Cruel or Cowardly."' DWM #508, cover date February 2017.

Cornell, Paul, 'Philip Martin Interview'. DWM #125, cover date June 1987.

Freeman, John, 'Talking to Tom Baker: Part Two'. DWM #180, cover date October 1991.

Hearn, Marcus, 'What The Papers Said'. DWM #204, cover date September 1993.

Hearn, Marcus, 'Writing Who: Pip and Jane Baker'. DWM #206, cover date November 1993.

Marson, Richard, 'Interview: John Nathan-Turner and Eric Saward'. DWM #108, cover date September 1985.

Marson, Richard, 'Chris Clough'. DWM #135, cover date April 1988.

Moffat, Steven, 'Production Notes.' DWM #457, cover date February 2013.

Marson, Richard, 'Pip and Jane Baker: Strange Matters'. DWM #137, cover date June 1988.

Nathan-Turner, John, 'This Must be the Place I waited Years to Leave' DWM #245, cover date November 1996.

Nathan-Turner, John, 'Listen, Do You Want to Know a Secret?' DWM #240, cover date July 1996.

Russell, Gary, 'Writing Doctor Who: Eric Saward'. DWM #148, cover date May 1989.

The Guardian.

Davies, Russell T, 'Have a Russell T Davies TV festival'. 1 January 2005.

Deans, Jason, 'Doctor Who Finally Makes the Grade'. 21 June 2005.

Stage and Television Today.

'Grade Slams Doctor Who Team'. 17 September 1985

Werson, Graham, 'Dr Who Chief Zapped By TV Script Editor'. 11 September 1986

The Sun.

Carroll, Sue, 'Why I'll Never Forgive Gutless Grade, by Axed Dr Who'. 6 January 1987.

Catchpole, Charles, 'Doctor Who Axed in Plot by the BBC'. 28 February 1985.

Time and Space Visualiser.

Scoones, Paul, 'The Trial of a Time Lord'. TSV 1, cover date July 1987.

The Times.

Hewson, David, 'BBC Keeps Option Of Killing Doctor Who'. 14 January 1986 (morning edition).

Hewson, David, 'BBC Doubts Over Future Of Doctor Who'. 14 January 1986 (evening edition).

'MPs Angry at BBC's New Buy'. *The Mail on Sunday*, 3 March 1985

Hill, Patrick, 'Dr Who Fails to Make the Grade'. *The Standard*, 27

March 1986.

Molesworth, Richard, 'Bob's Fantasy Factory'. *Nothing at the End of the Lane* #4, Autumn 2015.

Saward, Eric, 'The Revelations of a Script Editor'. *Starburst* #97, September 1986.

Stowell, Thomas, 'Jack the Ripper: A Solution?' *The Criminologist* vol 5 #9, November 1970.

Television

Breakfast Time. BBC, 1983-89.

Episode broadcast 28 February 1985.

Doctor Who. BBC, 1963-.

Paradise Towers

'Casting Sylvester'. DVD extra.

'Mindwarp', 1986.

DVD commentary.

'The Ultimate Foe', 1986.

DVD commentary.

'The Making of *The Trial of a Time Lord* Part 4: "The Ultimate Foe"'. DVD extra.

'Trials and Tribulations'. DVD extra.

'1985 Hiatus'. DVD extra.

Jack the Ripper. Thames, 1988.

The Lenny Henry Show. BBC, 1984-88, 1995, 2003-05.

> Episode broadcast 3 October 1985.

The Lively Arts. BBC, 1976-81.

> *Whose Doctor Who*, 1977.

Room 101. BBC, 1994-2007, 2012-.

> Episode broadcast 15 April 2002.

Star Trek. Desilu Productions, Norway Corporation, Paramount Television, 1966-69.

> *Wolf in the Fold*, 1967.

Wogan. BBC, 1982-1992.

> Episode broadcast 1 March 1985.

Film

Hooper, Tobe, dir, *The Texas Chainsaw Massacre*. Vortex, 1974.

Stage Plays

Pinter, Harold, *The Caretaker*. 1960.

Shakespeare, William, *Richard III*. 1594.

Audio CD

Nathan-Turner, John, *The John Nathan-Turner Memoirs*. Big Finish Productions, 2003. ISBN 9781844351435.

Web

'Albert Victor, Prince'. Oxford Dictionary of National Biography. http://www.oxforddnb.com/view/article/275 (subscription only).

Accessed 9 August 2017.

'An Interview with Colin Baker'. *The Whostorian Blog*, 22 August 2012. http://thewhostorian.blogspot.co.uk/2012/08/an-interview-with-colin-baker.html. Accessed 31 July 2017.

'Doctor Who Radio Int with Michael Grade BBC Radio 5, 9/4/08'. YouTube. https://www.youtube.com/watch?v=TalxgS19hAc. Accessed 6 August 2017.

'Michael Grade: "I Think The BBC Has Become Too Bureaucratic"'. *Radio Times*. http://www.radiotimes.com/news/2012-04-02/michael-grade-i-think-the-bbc-has-become-too-bureaucratic. Accessed 31 July 2017.

'Stephen, Sir James FitzJames, First Baronet'. Oxford Dictionary of National Biography, http://www.oxforddnb.com/view/article/26375/26376 (subscription only). Accessed 9 August 2017.

The Doctor Who Cuttings Archive. http://cuttingsarchive.org/index.php/Main_Page. Accessed 31 July 2017.

'The Ultimate Foe'. *The Doctor Who Ratings Guide*. http://pagefillers.com/dwrg/ulti.htm. Accessed 9 October 2017

BIOGRAPHY

James Cooray Smith is a freelance writer and critic whose credits include *The New Statesman, Prospect, Private Eye, Hero Collector* and *That Mitchell and Webb Sound*. He researched and wrote the production information subtitles for several official BBC **Doctor Who** DVD releases, and is the author of the well-received *The Black Archive #2: The Massacre*. He lives in North London with a Lady Barrister and their son, and can be found on twitter, usually talking about Doctor Who, as @thejimsmith.

Coming in 2018

The Black Archive #15: Carnival of Monsters by Ian Potter

The Black Archive #16: Full Circle by John Toon

The Black Archive #17: The Impossible Planet / The Satan Pit by Simon Bucher-Jones

The Black Archive #18: Marco Polo by Dene October

The Black Archive #19: The Eleventh Hour by Jon Arnold

The Black Archive #20: Face the Raven by Sarah Groenewegen

The Black Archive #21: Heaven Sent by Kara Dennison

The Black Archive #22: Hell Bent by Alyssa Franke

The Black Archive #23: The Curse of Fenric by Una McCormack

The Black Archive #24: The Time Warrior by Matthew Kilburn

The Black Archive #25: Doctor Who (1996) by Paul Driscoll

The Black Archive #26: The Dæmons by Matt Barber

CARNIVAL OF MONSTERS

Ian Potter

'Our purpose is to amuse… simply to amuse. Nothing serious, nothing political…'

Carnival of Monsters (1973) is a story of two halves. Two apparently unlinked stories unfold in a pair of quite different worlds. The crew of a steamship en route to Bombay in 1926 are menaced by a terror from the deep that should be extinct, while on an intensely socially stratified world, nervous officials prepare to make first contact with alien beings after thousands of years in isolation. Somehow, the Doctor and Jo Grant will find themselves stepping between these worlds in one of the most bizarre **Doctor Who** stories of its era.

Simultaneously a light comedy with satirical undercurrents and a thrilling children's adventure featuring ferocious alien beasts, *Carnival of Monsters* brings together a producer-director keen to push the boundaries of the electronic studio and a writer who delights in conjuring worlds from tiny off-stage details. The result is a remarkable piece of television with its own unique flavour that works on a number of levels for a variety of audiences.

Written with access to surviving scripts, storylines and production files this **Black Archive** volume explores the roots of *Carnival of Monsters* as a story, its thematic resonances and linguistic quirks and its occasionally troubled production. Roll up and see the monster show, and take a peek behind the curtain.

Available January 2018